Prentice Hall

MATHEMATICS

Test Prep

GRADE 7

Boston, Massachusetts • Chandler, Arizona • Glenview, Illinois • Upper Saddle River, New Jersey

ISBN-13: 978-0-13-372219-2
ISBN-10: 0-13-372219-8

4 5 6 7 8 9 10 V011 13 12

Table of Contents

Name ______________________ Class ______________ Date ______________

Writing Gridded Responses

Exercises

Write what you would grid for each answer. Then grid your answers on grids provided by your teacher.

1. Simplify 8(3.6). ______________
2. Find the sum of 4.23 and 8.43. ______________
3. Find the sum of 12.34 and 45.32. ______________
4. Find the difference between 6.8 and −3.4. ______________
5. Find $1\frac{1}{2} \div \frac{5}{8}$. ______________
6. Solve the proportion. $\frac{4}{12} = \frac{n}{6}$ ______________
7. Find the mean of the data set. 3 5 2 9 8 5 3 ______________
8. Find the next number in the sequence: 3, −6, 12, −24, ... ______________
9. To get to your grandfather's office, you have to walk up 8 flights of stairs each containing 10 steps. How many steps do you walk up?

    ____

10. You have $340 in a bank account. You have decided to add $8 per week to your account for the next seven weeks. What is your balance at the end of four weeks?

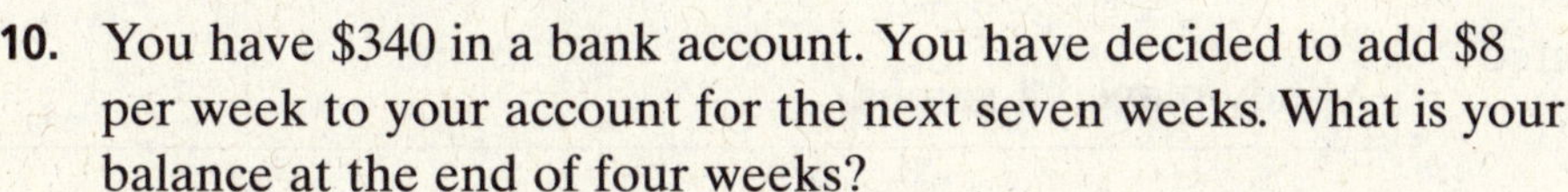

    ____

11. A carpenter cuts a 6-m board into 4 equal pieces. What is the length in centimeters of each piece?

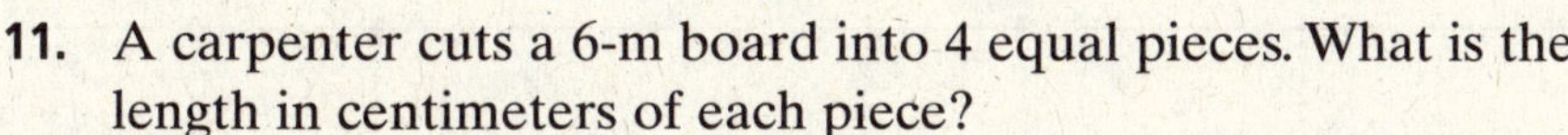

    ____

12. You spent $14.32 on scrapbook stickers. If each package of stickers cost $1.79, how many packages of stickers did you buy?

    ____

13. For your birthday you receive $30. If you buy a CD for $12.99 and a magazine for $4.95, how much money do you have left?

    ____

14. Software for Mr. Key's new computer costs the following: word processing $350, additional graphics $34.99, and tax software $79.99. What is the total cost of the software to the nearest dollar?

    ____

15. Margaret can type at a rate of 30 words per minute. At this rate, how long would it take her to type 450 words?

    ____

Name ______________________ Class ______________ Date ____________

Writing Short Responses

Exercises

Use the scoring rubric below to answer each question.

Scoring Rubric

- **2** The equation and the solution are correct.
- **1** There is no equation, but there is a method to show how the answer was achieved.
- **1** There is an equation and a solution, both of which may contain minor errors. The solution indicates the answer, but does not show units.
- **0** There is no response, it is completely incorrect, or it is the correct response but there is no procedure shown.

1. During a summer special, costs for bowling at the Swanton Sports Center are \$2.75 for shoe rental and \$1.50 for each game bowled. Mindy spent \$8.75. Write and solve an equation to find how many games she bowled.

2 points	1 point	0 points
Let $x =$ number of games. $2.75 + 1.50x = 8.75$ $1.50x = 6.00$ $\frac{1.50x}{1.50} = \frac{6.00}{1.50}$ $x = 4$ Mindy played 4 games.	$2.75 + 1.50x = 8.75$ $1.50x = 6.00$ $x = 9$ 9 games	3 games

a. Explain why each response above received the indicated points.

____

____

____

b. Write a 1-point response that does not have an equation.

____

2. While school shopping Marcus spent a total of \$63.93. His purchase included a new pair of jeans for \$21.99 and some T-shirts for \$6.99 each.

a. Write and solve an equation to find how many T-shirts he bought.

b. Write a 2-point response.

2 points	1 point	0 points
	$6.99t - 21.99 = 63.93$ $6.99t = 85.92$ $t = 12.29$ 12 T-shirts	7 T-shirts

Name ______________________ Class ______________ Date ______________

Reading for Understanding

Exercises

Use the passage to complete Exercises 1–4.

Cedar Point in Sandusky, Ohio, boasts one of the tallest roller coasters in the United States. The Millennium Force measures in at 310 feet. After riders reach the top of the first hill, they plunge 93 miles per hour down a 300-foot drop at an 80-degree angle. For the 2-minute, 20-second ride, riders are seated in one of three 36-passenger trains and travel along its 6,595-foot-long track.

1. How tall is the Millennium Force's tallest hill?

____

2. How many seconds does each ride take?

____

3. The three trains together can complete about 44 rides in an hour. How many passengers can ride in one hour?

____

4. How many miles long is the track? (Hint: 5,280 feet = 1 mile)

____

Use the passage to complete Exercises 5–7.

The giraffe is one of the heaviest land animals. Large males can weigh up to 1,900 kg. Females are smaller and rarely reach half the weight of the males. A giraffe's neck and long legs combine to make the giraffe one of the tallest of all animals, averaging about 17 feet tall for a male. The giraffe's neck, supported by seven elongated vertebrae, can measure even longer than its 1.8-m (6-ft) legs. A giraffe's long legs give it the ability to run at a top speed of about 56 km/h (35 mi/h).

5. What is the weight of a large giraffe in pounds? (Hint: There are 2.2 pounds per kilogram.)

____

6. What is the weight of a female giraffe, in kilograms?

____

7. How far could a giraffe travel at its top speed in fifteen minutes?

____

Name ______________________ Class ______________ Date ____________

Writing Extended Responses

Exercises

Use the scoring rubric shown to answer each question.

Scoring Rubric

4 Identifies the variables, shows all work, and answers all parts of the problem.

3 Identifies the variable, shows work, and answers all parts of the problem. There may be a computational error.

1 Problem set up incorrectly, does not answer all parts of the problem and contains errors.

1. Parts to fix your truck cost you \$115.95. The mechanic charges \$42 per hour for labor. The final bill you receive is \$241.95. How long did the mechanic work on your truck? Write and solve an equation. Show all your work.

4 points	3 points
Let h = hours worked. $42h + 115.95 = 241.95$ $42h + 115.95 - 115.95 = 241.95 - 115.95$ $42h = 126$ $\frac{42h}{42} = \frac{126}{42}$ $h = 3$ The mechanic worked a total of 3 hours on the truck.	Let h = hours worked. $42h + 115.95 = 241.95$ $42h = 357.90$ $\frac{42h}{42} = \frac{357.90}{42}$ $h = 8.5$ 8.5 hours

a. Read the 3-point response. What error was made?

____

____

b. Write what you think a 2-point response to the problem would look like.

____

2. Aaron works at Hobby Town and has 256 purple bracelet beads and 96 orange bracelet beads to repackage. Each new bag must contain the same number of purple beads and the same number of orange beads. Aaron wants to make as many bags as possible. How many bags can he make? How many beads of each color will Aaron put in each new bag?

a. Write a 4-point response to the problem.

____

____

____

b. Write a 1-point response to the problem.

____

Name ______________________ Class ______________ Date ______________

Using a Variable

Exercises

Use a variable to write an equation and solve each problem.

1. A lunch platter contains a variety of luncheon meats. To serve 12 people, $3\frac{1}{2}$ pounds of meat are needed. How many pounds of meat are needed to serve 18 people?

____

2. If 80 kg of cement are used to make 400 kg of concrete, how much cement is needed to make 1,600 kg of concrete?

____

3. A machine produces 2,070 flashlights in 8.5 hours. How many flashlights will the machine produce in 40 hours?

____

4. You receive $72.96 for working an 8-hour day. How much would you receive for working a 32-hour week?

____

5. A clothing manufacturer is shipping sweaters to a department store. The manufacturer has previously shipped 330 sweaters in 18 boxes. At this rate, how many boxes would the manufacturer need to ship 550 sweaters?

____

6. The monthly payment on a loan is $29.50 for every $1,000 borrowed. At this rate, find the monthly payment for a $9,000 car loan.

____

7. Nine ceramic tiles are required to cover four square feet. At this rate, how many square feet can be tiled with 270 ceramic tiles?

____

8. A quality control inspector found three defective computer chips in a shipment of 500 chips. At this rate, how many computer chips would be defective in a shipment of 3,000 chips?

____

9. The ratio of chicory to coffee in a New England coffee mixture is 1 : 8. If the coffee company uses 85 pounds of chicory for a batch of coffee mixture, how many pounds of coffee are needed?

____

10. In preparing a banquet for 30 people, a restaurant cook uses nine pounds of potatoes. How many pounds of potatoes will be needed for a banquet for 175 people?

____

Name ______________________ Class ______________ Date ______________

Working Backward

Exercises

Solve each problem by working backward. Circle the correct answer.

1. Your grades on five math tests are 95, 86, 79, 88, and 93. What grade do you need on the sixth test to have an average of 90?

   A. 76 **B.** 90 **C.** 99 **D.** 100

2. The surface area of a cube is 294 square feet. What is the length (in feet) of each edge of the cube? [Hint: $S = 6s^2$]

   F. -7 feet **G.** 7 feet **H.** 49 feet **J.** 64 feet

3. If $7x - 17 = 32$, what is the value of x?

   A. 2.14 **B.** 5 **C.** 7 **D.** 9

4. What is the greatest number of theater tickets you can buy if you have $227.18 and each theater ticket costs $42.75?

   F. 4 tickets **G.** 5 tickets **H.** 6 tickets **J.** 7 tickets

5. If you start with a number, multiply by 3, then subtract 16, the result is 152. What is the number?

   A. 37 **B.** 48 **C.** 51 **D.** 56

6. A CD player is on sale for $54.99. The CD player has been discounted 25%. What is the original price of the CD player?

   F. $13.75 **G.** $68.74 **H.** $73.32 **J.** $75.00

7. If $\frac{3}{8} = \frac{x}{32}$, then x = ______.

   A. 4 **B.** 12 **C.** 24 **D.** 96

8. The formula for the area of a triangle is $A = \frac{1}{2}bh$. If the area of a triangle is 48 square feet and the height is 6 feet, what is the length of the base?

   F. 12 feet **G.** 16 feet **H.** 24 feet **J.** 48 feet

9. Juan can buy one ice cream cone for $.90. What is the greatest number of ice cream cones he can buy for $6.00?

   A. 3 cones **B.** 4 cones **C.** 5 cones **D.** 6 cones

10. A train left New York at 1:20 A.M. and reached its stop $3\frac{1}{4}$ hours later. What time did the train reach its stop?

    F. 4:35 A.M. **G.** 4:45 A.M. **H.** 5:20 A.M. **J.** 6:00 A.M.

11. If $\frac{x}{8} = 114$, what is the value of x?

    A. 14.25 **B.** 112 **C.** 812 **D.** 912

Name ______________________ Class ______________ Date ______________

Drawing a Picture

Exercises

Draw a diagram to solve each exercise.

1. $\triangle ABC \cong \triangle DEF$. The measure of $\angle A = 51°$, and the measure of $\angle C = 94°$. What is the measure of $\angle E$?

   ____

2. On a bus line, three towns are represented by points *G, H,* and *J*. Town *G* is 55 miles north of Town *H*, and Town *J* is 10 mi south of Town *G*. Which town is between the other two?

   ____

3. The angle bisector of one angle of a triangle measures 42°. The angle bisector of another angle of the triangle measures 36°. What is the measure of the third angle of the triangle?

   ____

4. Team *L* and Team *M* have a tug of war. From their starting positions Team *L* pulls Team *M* forward 3 meters, and Team *L* is then pulled forward 5 meters. Team *M* then pulls Team *L* forward 4 meters. If the first team to be pulled forward 10 meters loses, how many more meters must Team *M* pull Team *L* forward to win?

   ____

5. On a number line point *A* is 5 units to the left of point *B*. Point *A* is located at coordinate -7.2. What is the coordinate of point *B*?

   ____

6. Circle *M* has a diameter of 12 inches. Radii $\overline{MN}$ and $\overline{MP}$ form an angle that is not a straight angle. The length of $\overline{NP}$ is *not* 12 inches. Classify $\triangle MNP$ according to its sides.

   ____

7. During a sightseeing tour in Washington D.C., the tour bus travels 4 blocks due north, 6 blocks due east, 12 blocks due south, 22 blocks due west, and 8 blocks due north. At this point, where is the tour bus in relation to its starting point?

   ____

8. How many diagonals can be drawn in a hexagon?

   ____

9. Rectangle *ABCD* has a perimeter of 62. If the length of $\overline{AD}$ is 14, what is the area of *ABCD*?

   ____

Name ______________________________ Class ____________________ Date ______________

Measuring to Solve

Exercises

Use a ruler to answer each question.

1. The bottom of a soup can is circular, as shown at the right. Measure the radius of the circle in centimeters. Find the circumference of the circle. Use 3.14 for π.

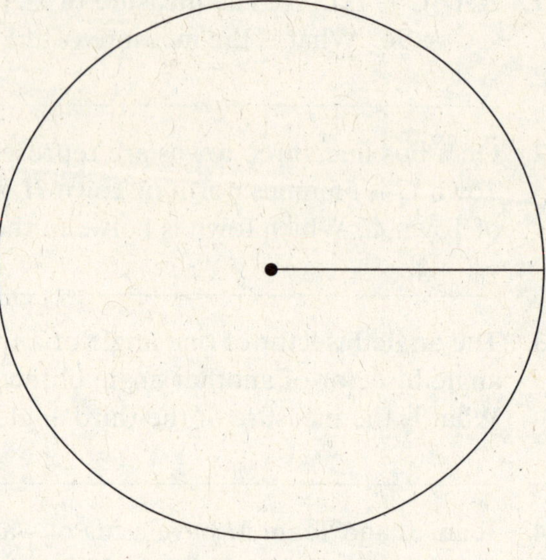

____

2. The front of a box of cereal is a rectangle, as shown at the right. Measure the dimensions of the rectangle in centimeters. Find the perimeter of the rectangle.

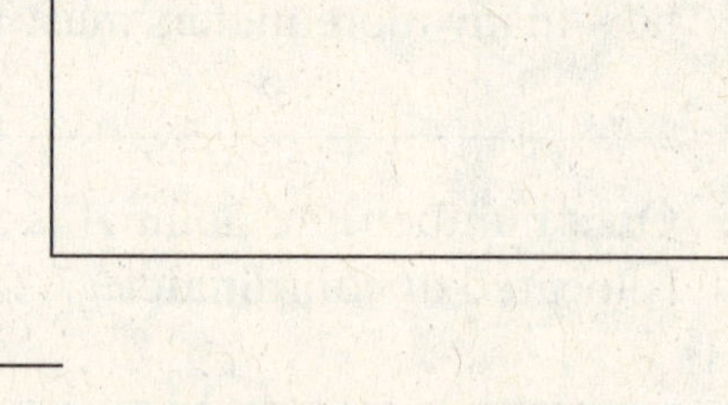

____

3. A box of tea bags is a cube. The top of the box is the square shown at the right. Measure the dimensions of the square. Find the area of the square.

____

Name ______________________ Class ______________ Date ______________

Estimating the Answer

Exercises

Estimate each answer. Circle the letter of the best answer.

1. The circumference of a circle is about 24 ft. Which is closest to the length of the diameter of the circle?

   A. 8 ft **B.** 9 ft **C.** 10 ft **D.** 11 ft

2. Farmer's Merchantile is offering a 30% discount on all farm gates. Which is closest to the discount price of a farm gate that regularly costs $130?

   F. $40 **G.** $90 **H.** $100 **J.** $120

3. The lengths of two legs of a right triangle are 5 ft and 10 ft. Which is closest to the length of the hypotenuse?

   A. 10 ft **B.** 11 ft **C.** 13 ft **D.** 15.5 ft

4 Which is the best estimate for the mean of the data set? 30, 34, 25, 30, 38, 32

   F. 40 **G.** 35 **H.** 30 **J.** 25

5. You borrow $500 at a 4% simple interest rate. About how much interest will you owe in 2 years?

   A. $20 **B.** $40 **C.** $80 **D.** $520

6. On Friday, $\frac{5}{9}$ of the students at school bought pizza for lunch. About what percent of the students did *not* buy pizza for lunch?

   F. 35% **G.** 45% **H.** 55% **J.** 65%

7. Four pieces of trim, each $8\frac{1}{2}$-inches long are cut from a board 100 inches long. About how many inches of board remain?

   A. 34 inches **B.** 50 inches **C.** 66 inches **D.** 75 inches

8. Linden bought a jacket for 15% off the regular retail price of $110. What did Linden pay for the jacket?

   F. $16.50 **G.** $65.60 **H.** $75.80 **J.** $93.50

Name ______________________ Class ______________ Date ______________

Answering the Question Asked

Exercises

Use the table below to answer exercises 1–4.

Record Breakers

What	Name	Size
Deepest Lake	Baikal	5,315 feet deep
Largest Continent	Asia	17,212,041 square miles
Lowest Land Point	Dead Sea	1,349 feet below sea level
Largest Gorge	Grand Canyon	277 miles long, up to 18 miles wide, 1 mile deep
Longest Mountain Range	Andes	more than 5,000 miles
Longest River	Nile	4,145 miles
Shortest River	Roe	201 feet

1. What is the longest river?
   A. Nile **B.** Roe **C.** Andes **D.** Baikal

2. What is the difference between the longest and shortest river, in feet?
   F. 3,944 feet **G.** 4,346 feet **H.** 2,189 feet **J.** 2.189×10^7 feet

3. At its widest point, what is the volume of the Grand Canyon?
   A. 4,986 miles^3 **B.** 3,256 miles^3 **C.** 296 miles^3 **D.** 295 miles^3

4. What is the difference in length between the longest mountain range and the longest river?
   F. 300 miles **G.** 855 miles **H.** 1,000 miles **J.** 2,290 miles

Use the double bar graph for exercises 5–7.

5. Which of the following continents had the least amount of change in wheat production per 1,000 capita between 1961 and 2000?
   A. Africa **B.** Asia
   C. North America **D.** South America

6. What is the approximate change in Europe's wheat production per 1,000 capita from 1961 to 2000?
   F. 100 tons **G.** 150 tons
   H. 170 tons **J.** 200 tons

7. In 2000, what is the approximate mean of wheat produced for all continents shown?
   A. 200 tons **B.** 250 tons
   C. 300 tons **D.** 350 tons

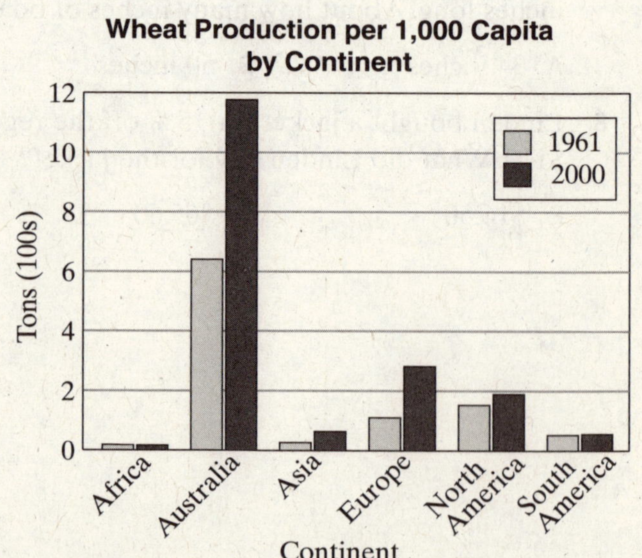

Name ______________________ Class ______________ Date ______________

Interpreting Data

Exercises

Use the graphs at the right to answer each question.

Scores on Science Test

Stem	Leaf
9	0 0 1 3 5 7 7 8
8	0 1 1 1 2 3 6 8 8 9
7	6 8 8 9
6	7

Key: 9 | 0 means 90

1. What is the median of the scores shown in the stem-and-leaf plot at the right?

   A. 6 **B.** 8 **C.** 81 **D.** 86

2. What is the range of the scores shown in the stem-and-leaf plot at the right?

   F. 9 **G.** 23 **H.** 31 **J.** 86

Votes for New Mascot Name

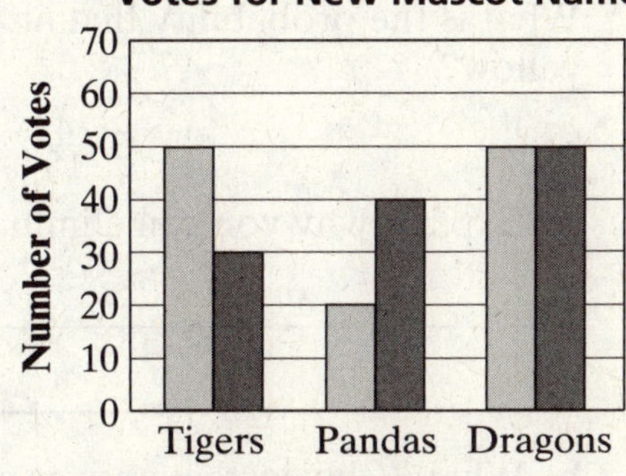

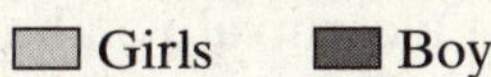

3. Which statement is best supported by the information in the bar graph at the right?

   A. More girls voted for "Pandas" than voted for "Tigers."

   B. The total number of votes for "Pandas" was the same as the total number of votes for "Dragons."

   C. The same number of girls voted for "Dragons" as voted for "Tigers."

   D. The fewest number of votes went to "Tigers."

Riley's Drive to Work

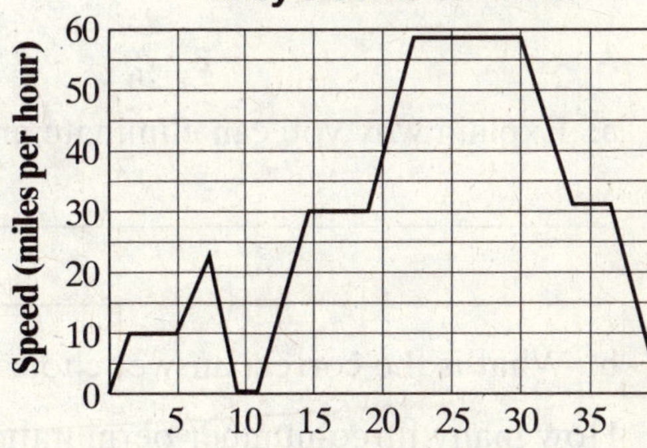

4. Which statement is NOT supported by the information in the line graph at the right?

   F. It took Riley approximately 40 minutes to drive to work.

   G. Riley's maximum speed on the way to work is about 58 miles per hour.

   H. Riley stops 4 times on his way to work.

   J. Riley's maximum speed for the first 10 minutes of the drive is about 20 miles per hour.

Name ________________ Class ________________ Date ________________

Eliminating Answers

Exercises

Solve each problem.

1. A quality-control inspector found 40 defective crayons out of 1,000 that she checked. What percent of the crayons were defective?

   A. 400% **B.** 100% **C.** 40% **D.** 4%

   a. Explain why you can eliminate answer choices A and C.

   ____

   b. What is the correct answer choice? ________________

2. A bag contains 6 green apples, 8 red apples, and 16 yellow apples. What is the probability that an apple selected at random is yellow?

   F. $\frac{1}{8}$ **G.** $\frac{4}{15}$ **H.** $\frac{8}{15}$ **J.** 1

   a. Explain why you can eliminate answer choices F and J.

   ____

   ____

   b. What is the correct answer choice? ________________

3. At a carnival you have the chance to spin the letter wheel. The letter wheel has 26 spaces, each with a different letter of the alphabet. You spin the spinner twice. Find $P(C, \text{then } H)$.

   A. $\frac{1}{2}$ **B.** $\frac{1}{26}$ **C.** $\frac{1}{52}$ **D.** $\frac{1}{676}$

   a. Explain why you can eliminate answer choices A and B.

   ____

   ____

   b. What is the correct answer choice? ________________

4. How many three-number permutations can be formed from the numbers 1, 2, 3, 4, and 5, if no digit is used more than once?

   F. 240 **G.** 120 **H.** 60 **J.** 30

   a. Explain why you can eliminate answer choices F and G.

   ____

   ____

   b. What is the correct answer choice? ________________

Name ______________________ Class ______________ Date ______________

NAEP Practice Test

1. Lindsay needs to buy 12 cans of tomato sauce to make spaghetti for her family. Each can of spaghetti sauce costs \$0.89. Which expression gives Lindsay the most accurate estimation of the total cost of 12 cans?

   A \$2 × 12

   B \$1 × 12

   C \$0.75 × 12

   D \$0.50 × 12

   E \$0.25 × 12

2. Between which two consecutive whole numbers does $\sqrt{58}$ lie?

   A 4 and 5

   B 5 and 6

   C 6 and 7

   D 7 and 8

   E 8 and 9

3. Jill is going to run a 5 kilometer race. If 1 kilometer is approximately $\frac{5}{8}$ mile, how many miles long is the race?

   A $2\frac{1}{2}$ miles

   B 3 miles

   C $3\frac{1}{8}$ miles

   D 5 miles

   E 8 miles

4. At the football team's end of the year banquet, there were five pies to choose from for dessert. The shaded region of each circle shows how much pie was left over. Which pie had the most left over?

   A

   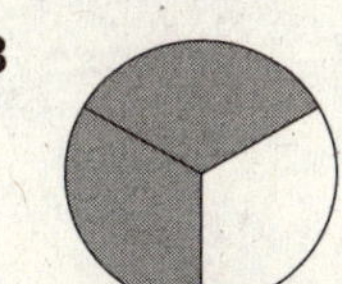

   B

   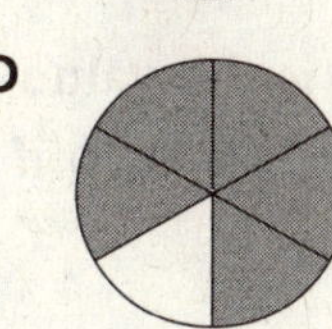

   C

   D

   E

5. Which data set has the median with the greatest value?

   A 2, 3, 2, 3, 7, 7, 5, 6, 3

   B 2, 2, 3, 2, 4, 7, 5, 6, 6

   C 3, 3, 2, 6, 7, 6, 7, 7, 4

   D 3, 4, 6, 3, 2, 7, 5, 6, 5

   E 4, 3, 4, 7, 3, 4, 6, 5, 2

6. Jack's last six test scores are 75, 78, 83, 80, 79, and 84. If he scores a 90 on the next test, by how much will his mean test score increase? Round to the nearest hundredth.

   A 1.45

   B 8.30

   C 14.50

   D 79.80

   E 81.30

GO ON

7. Jerry has 3 less than 4 times as many baseball cards as his little brother. Which expression represents the number of baseball cards Jerry has?

A v

B $7v$

C $3v - 7$

D $4v - 3$

E $3v - 4$

8. What is the value of the expression $ab^2 + 3(a - b)$ if $a = 3$ and $b = -2$?

A 3

B 13

C 27

D 37

E 51

9. There are 192 people going on a field trip to the museum. If one bus seats 32 people, which equation can be used to find the number of buses needed for the trip?

A $32x = 192$

B $192x = 32$

C $32 + x = 192$

D $\frac{x}{192} = 32$

E $\frac{x}{32} = 192$

10. Solve for w.

$w - 3 = -8$

A -11

B -5

C $2\frac{2}{3}$

D 11

E 24

11. Jim and Beth are trying to solve the equation $7 - x = 25$. Jim says that if they just subtract 7 from both sides, they will be finished. What should Beth say to Jim to prove him wrong?

A No, what we need to do is add 7 to both sides.

B No, what we need to do is add x to both sides.

C No, we should add 7 to both sides and then divide both sides by -1.

D No, we should subtract 7 from both sides and then divide both sides by -1.

E No, we should add x to both sides and then add 7 to both sides.

12. Solve for x.

$3x + 6 = 7$

A -3

B $-\frac{1}{3}$

C $\frac{1}{3}$

D 3

E $4\frac{1}{3}$

Name __________ Class __________ Date __________

13. Which equation represents the model?

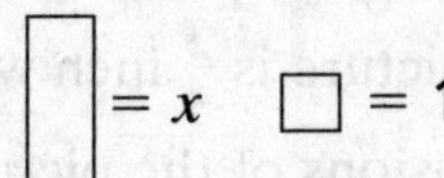

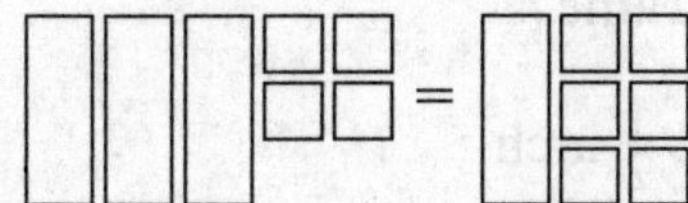

A $7x = 7$

B $3x + 4 = 7$

C $4x + 3 = 6x + 1$

D $3x - 4 = x - 6$

E $3x + 4 = x + 6$

14. Which inequality represents the graph?

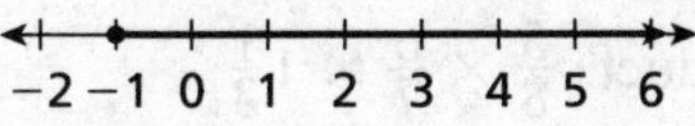

A $x > -1$

B $x \geq -1$

C $x < -1$

D $x \leq -1$

E $x = -1$

15. Which of the following is NOT a solution for the inequality $r - 8 > 16$?

A 24

B 25

C 26

D 27

E 28

16. If $\frac{x}{-6} \leq 12$, then

A $x \leq -72$.

B $x \geq -72$.

C $x \leq -2$.

D $x \geq -2$.

E $x \leq 72$.

17. The table lists the distance from each planet to the Sun. What is the distance between the two planets that are furthest from the Sun?

Planet	Distance from Sun (in kilometers)
Saturn	1.49×10^8 km
Neptune	4.50×10^9 km
Venus	1.08×10^8 km
Jupiter	7.78×10^8 km
Uranus	2.87×10^9 km

A 7.37×10^9 km

B 1.63×10^8 km

C 3.28×10^7 km

D 1.70×10^{10} km

E 1.63×10^9 km

18. Hilary is making holiday gift bags for all the children she baby-sits. She has 126 toys. Of the choices listed below, what is the most bags she can make if each bag has an equal number of toys in it?

A 2

B 3

C 5

D 9

E 10

GO ON

19. What is the largest prime factor of 924?

A 2

B 3

C 4

D 7

E 11

20. Which fraction, when simplified, does NOT equal $\frac{2}{3}$?

A $\frac{4}{6}$

B $\frac{10}{15}$

C $\frac{18}{20}$

D $\frac{24}{36}$

E $\frac{30}{45}$

21. An earthworm moves $\frac{5}{8}$ inch one minute and $\frac{3}{4}$ inch the next minute. What is the total distance the earthworm traveled in these two minutes?

A $\frac{1}{2}$ inch

B $\frac{8}{12}$ inch

C 1 inch

D $1\frac{1}{12}$ inch

E $1\frac{3}{8}$ inch

22. A picture measures $5\frac{1}{8}$ inch by $10\frac{1}{4}$ inch. The frame for the picture is $\frac{3}{4}$ inch wide. What are the dimensions of the picture, including the frame?

A $7\frac{3}{8}$ inch by $9\frac{1}{2}$ inch

B $6\frac{5}{8}$ inch by $11\frac{3}{4}$ inch

C $6\frac{1}{4}$ inch by $11\frac{3}{4}$ inch

D $4\frac{1}{8}$ inch by $10\frac{1}{4}$ inch

E $5\frac{1}{8}$ inch by $9\frac{1}{4}$ inch

23. Find the product. $\frac{5}{8} \times \frac{6}{7} \times 1\frac{1}{3}$

A $\frac{5}{28}$

B $\frac{45}{112}$

C $\frac{5}{7}$

D $\frac{15}{28}$

E $1\frac{2}{5}$

24. Find the quotient. $4\frac{1}{5} \div 1\frac{2}{5}$

A $1\frac{1}{5}$

B $1\frac{3}{5}$

C 3

D 4

E $5\frac{22}{25}$

GO ON

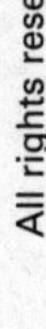

25. Harry is measuring the width of the street in front of his house. Which unit of measurement should be used?

A millimeters

B inches

C meters

D miles

E kilometers

26. On the first day of a hike, Mary hiked 3.25 kilometers. On the second day, she hiked 2.1 kilometers. What is the best estimate, to the nearest whole kilometer, of the total distance that Mary hiked?

A 1.05 km

B 5 km

C 5.55 km

D 5.6 km

E 6 km

27. Which figure has the largest *shaded* area to *non-shaded* area ratio?

A 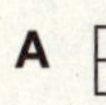

B 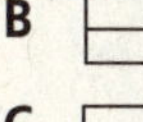

C

D

E 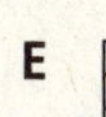

28. A train can travel 147 miles in 3 hours. How many miles can the train travel in 1 hour?

A 43 miles

B 49 miles

C 50 miles

D 57 miles

E 441 miles

29. Mr. Carlson is grading quizzes on solving proportions. Which response correctly used cross products to solve the proportion $\frac{15}{x} = \frac{6}{4}$?

A $15 = 6x$

B $15 = 24x$

C $(6)(4) = 15x$

D $(15)(4) = 6x$

E $(6)(15) = 4x$

30. If $\frac{16}{21} = \frac{x}{14}$, then $x =$

A $10\frac{2}{3}$.

B $18\frac{3}{8}$.

C 24.

D 32.

E 42.

GO ON

31. A tree with a height of 8-ft has a shadow 6-ft long. At the same time of day, a nearby building has a 16-ft shadow. How tall is the building?

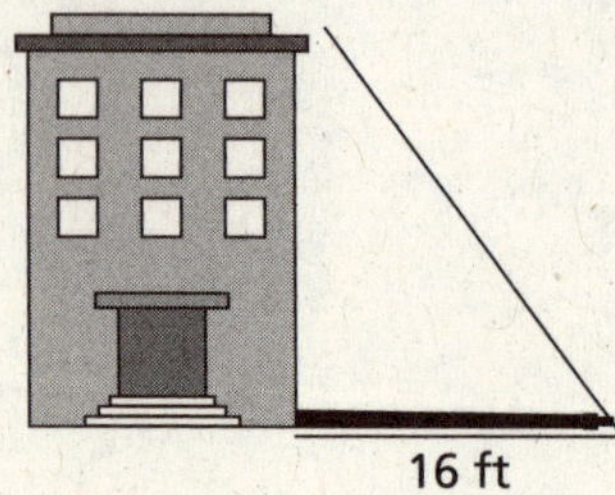

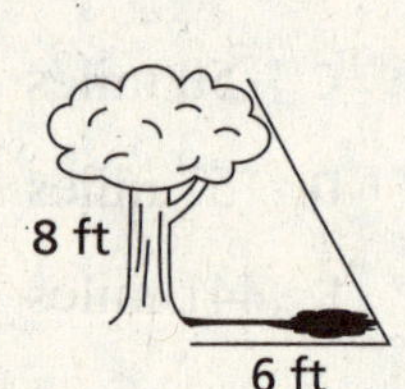

A 3 ft

B 12 ft

C $21\frac{1}{3}$ ft

D $24\frac{2}{3}$ ft

E 32 ft

32. The model car below has a scale of 1 inch = $2\frac{1}{2}$ feet. What is the length of the actual car?

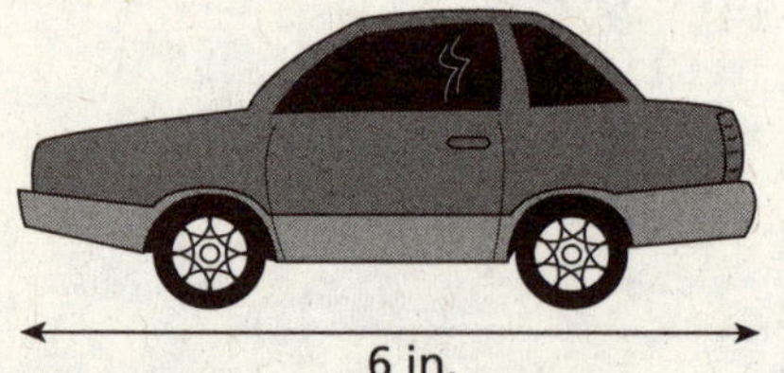

A 2.4 ft

B 4.5 ft

C 8.5 ft

D 15.0 ft

E 16.0 ft

33. An architect is drawing a blueprint of a house that is being remodeled. The scale is 1 cm = 1.5 m. If the dimensions of the actual kitchen are 9 m × 6 m, what is the area of the kitchen on the blueprint?

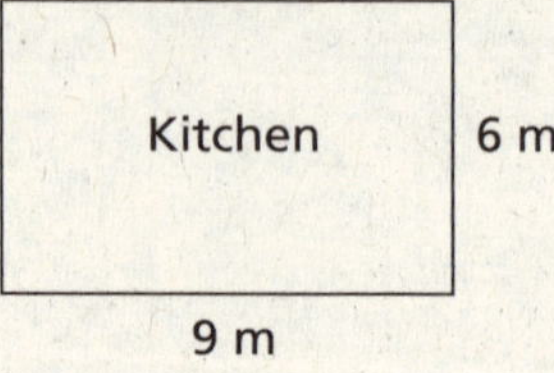

A 12 cm^2

B 18 cm^2

C 24 cm^2

D 27 cm^2

E 54 cm^2

34. Annie bought the items below and received a 25% discount off the regular price of each item. The sales tax in Annie's state is 6.5%. What is the total that Annie paid for these items, including sales tax?

A $23.74

B $71.23

C $75.86

D $94.97

E $126.43

Name ______________________ Class ______________ Date ______________

35. Kory scored 36 points out of a possible 40 points. What percent of the possible points did Kory score?

A 5%

B 35%

C 70%

D 90%

E 142%

36. Eight hundred students ride the bus to school. This is 25% of the school's student population. How many students attend the school?

A 200

B 1,000

C 1,800

D 3,200

E 3,800

37. A store manager buys leather wallets for $12 and then marks the price up 250%. How much does the manager sell the wallets for?

A $30

B $42

C $60

D $250

E $262

38. In which figure is the measure of $\angle CBD$ equal to 45°?

A

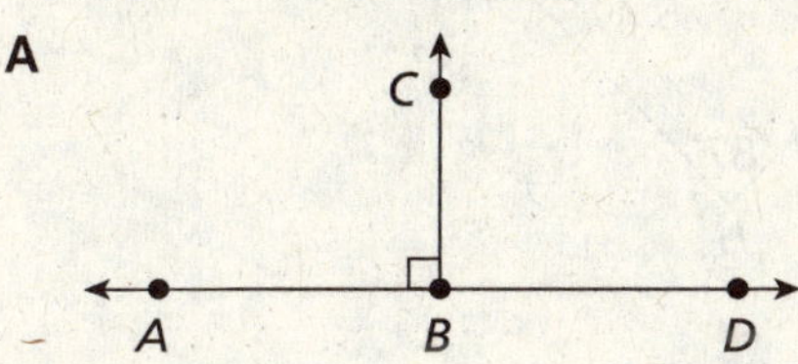

B

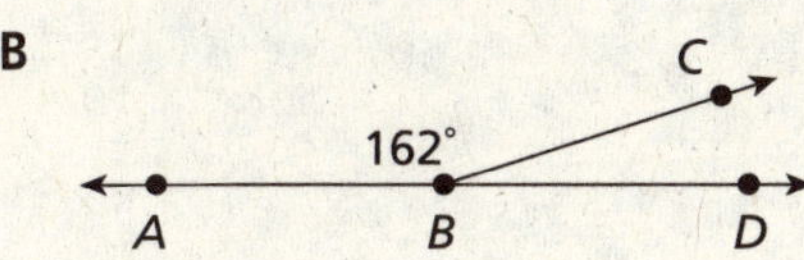

C

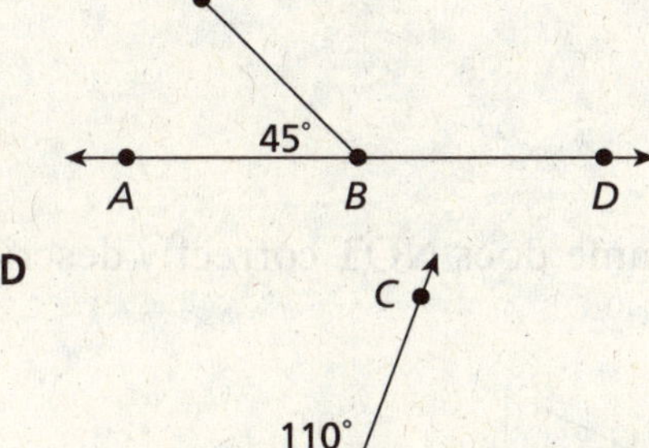

D

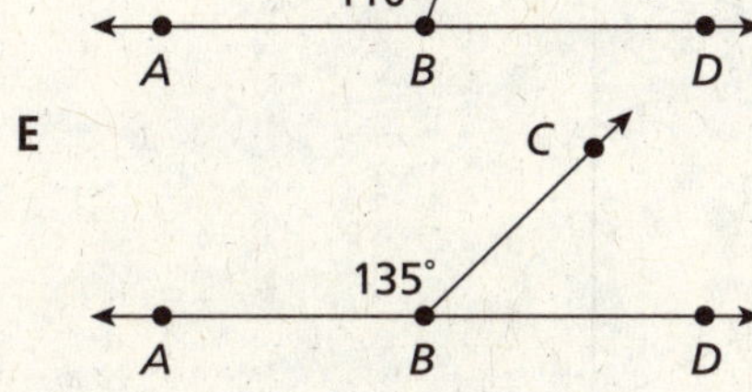

E

39. Which triangle is a right isosceles triangle?

A

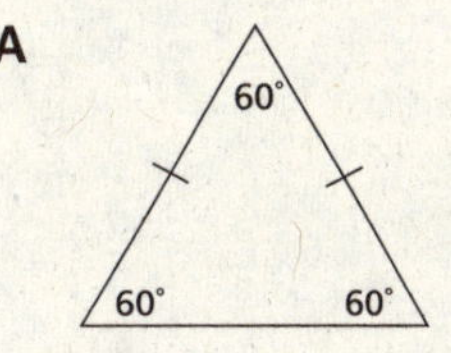

B

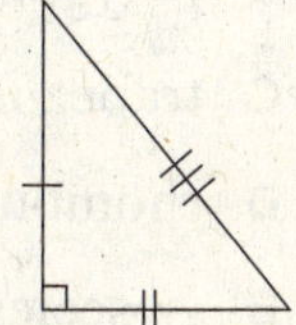

C

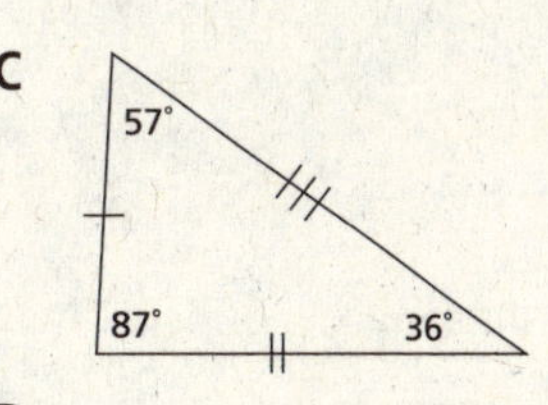

D

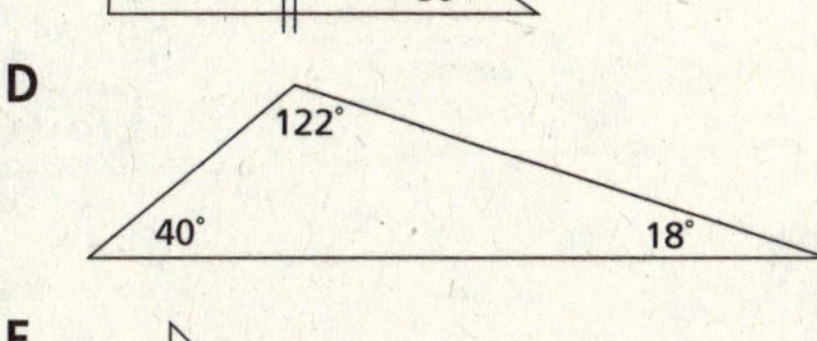

E

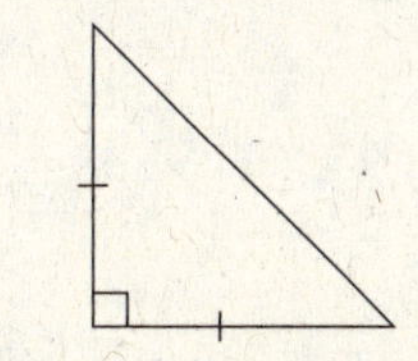

40. What is the measure of $\angle F$?

F G 47° 87° H

A 24°

B 46°

C 47°

D 90°

E 134°

41. Which name does NOT correctly describe the figure?

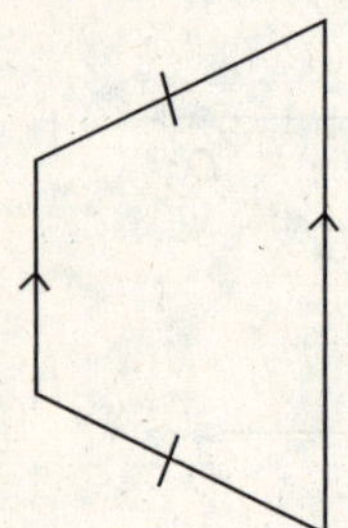

A quadrilateral

B polygon

C trapezoid

D rhombus

E isosceles

42. Which polygon has four congruent sides, no right angles, and opposite sides parallel?

A

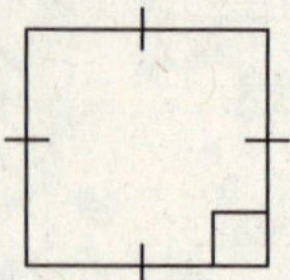

B

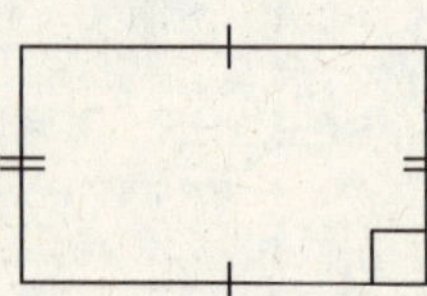

C

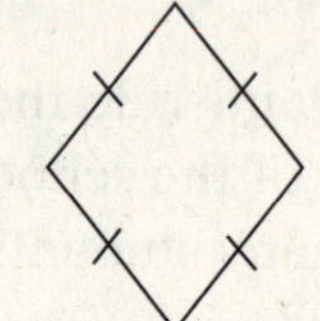

D

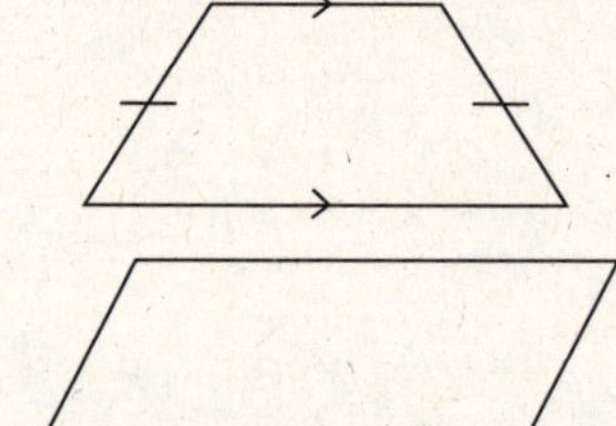

E

43. A square can be classified as all of the following except:

A a polygon.

B a triangle.

C a rectangle.

D a rhombus.

E a quadrilateral.

GO ON

44. What is the sum of the angle measures of the figure?

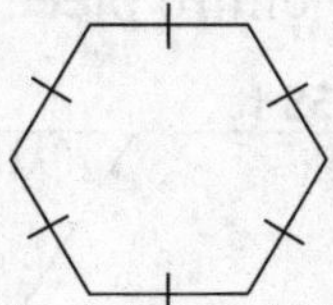

A 180°

B 360°

C 540°

D 720°

E 900°

45. What is *DE*, to the nearest tenth of a centimeter?

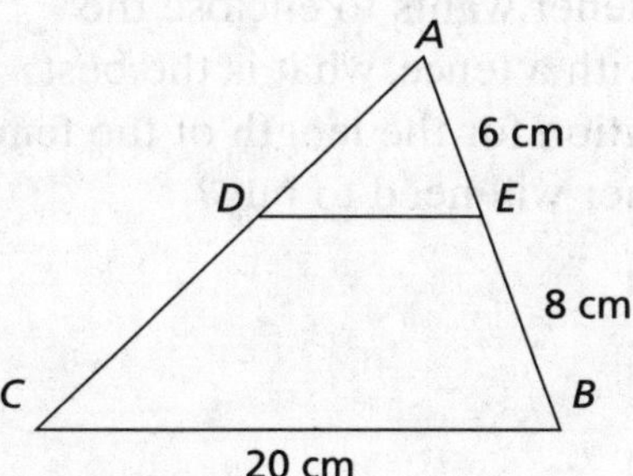

A 8.6 cm

B 10.2 cm

C 15.0 cm

D 18.0 cm

E 26.7 cm

46. What is the radius of circle *P*?

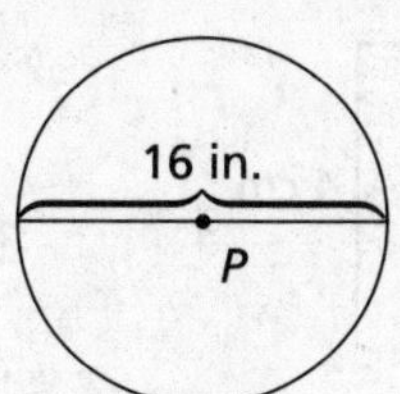

A 4 inches

B 8 inches

C 16 inches

D 20 inches

E 24 inches

47. If 200 students participate in extracurricular activities, how many play football?

Student Participation in Extracurricular Activities

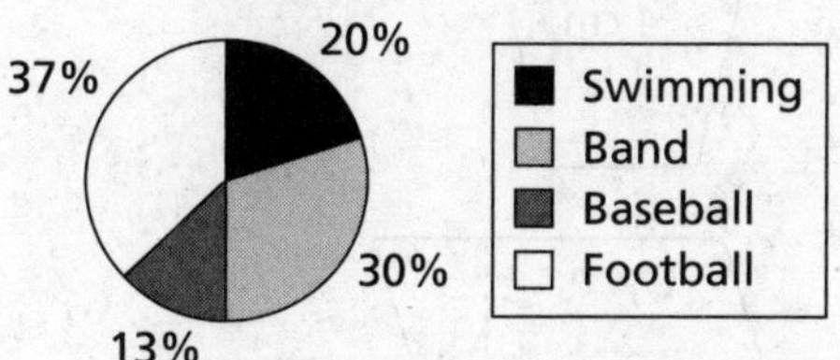

A 26 students

B 40 students

C 60 students

D 74 students

E 120 students

GO ON

48. Which figure has the smallest area?

A

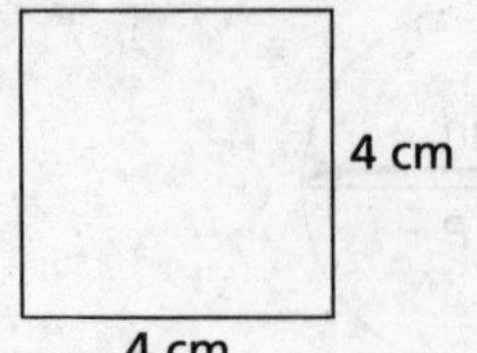

B

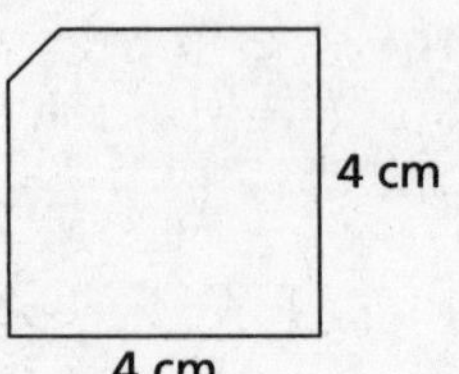

C

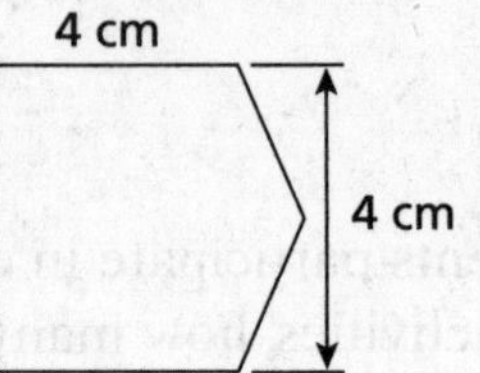

D

E

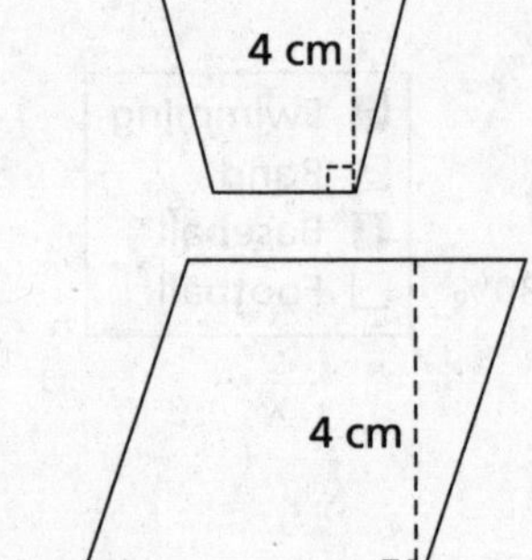

49. A child is using sidewalk chalk to draw a triangular-shaped area for a game. If the height of the area is twice the base, and the base is 6 feet, what is the area of the game?

A 12 ft^2

B 36 ft^2

C 72 ft^2

D 84 ft^2

E 120 ft^2

50. A parcel of land is for sale. It is priced at \$100 per square foot. Use the figure shown to find the cost of the entire piece of land.

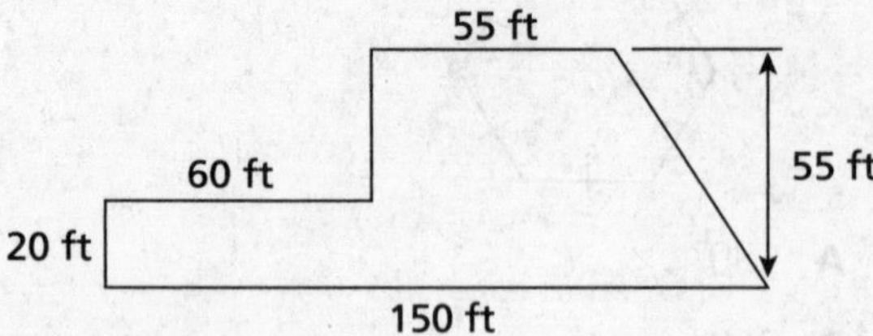

A \$518.75

B \$1050.50

C \$5187.50

D \$39,500.00

E \$518,750.00

51. A circular fountain has a radius of 10 feet. If the gardener wants to enclose the fountain with a fence, what is the best approximation for the length of the fence the gardener will need to buy?

A 20 feet

B 36 feet

C 63 feet

D 100 feet

E 314 feet

52. A boat's sail is 6 meters long and 8 meters high. What is the length of the diagonal of the sail?

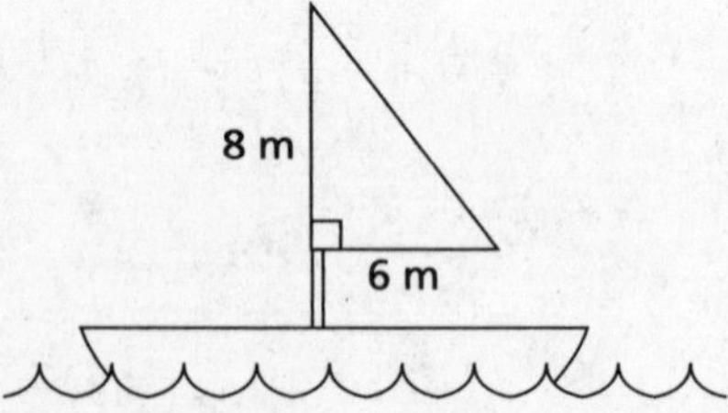

A 10 meters

B 13 meters

C 25 meters

D 100 meters

E 121 meters

53. A silo has a diameter of 3 meters and a height of 8 meters. Approximately, how much grain does the silo hold?

A 38 m^3

B 57 m^3

C 75 m^3

D 153 m^3

E 226 m^3

54. If the pattern in the list below continues, what will be the next number after 31?

16, 23, 20, 27, 24, 31, . . .

A 25

B 28

C 33

D 38

E 41

55. Which operation should you use to get the next number in the pattern?

8, 11, 14, 17, . . .

A Take the square root.

B Multiply by 3.

C Add 3.

D Subtract 3.

E Divide by 3.

56. Which rule represents the graph of the points shown on the coordinate plane?

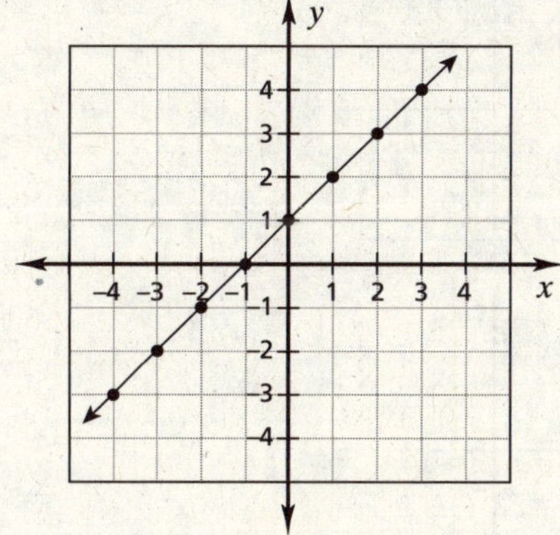

A $y = -x$

B $y = x - 1$

C $y = x + 1$

D $y = -x - 1$

E $y = -x + 1$

57. Which of the following ordered pairs is a solution of the equation $3x - 4y = 12$?

A (4, 6)

B (3, 4)

C (0, 3)

D (−4, 0)

E (−4, −6)

58. The line passing through which two pair of points has the steepest slope?

A (1, 2) and (5, −2)

B (2, −4) and (3, 0)

C (2, 5) and (−3, 6)

D (−2, 1) and (5, 6)

E (−1, 2) and (0, 4)

59. Which is a graph of a linear function?

A

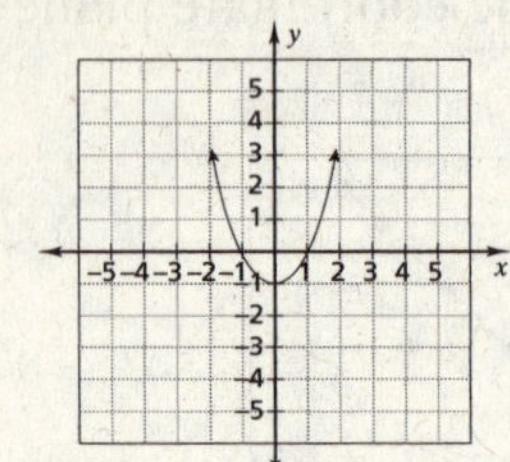

B

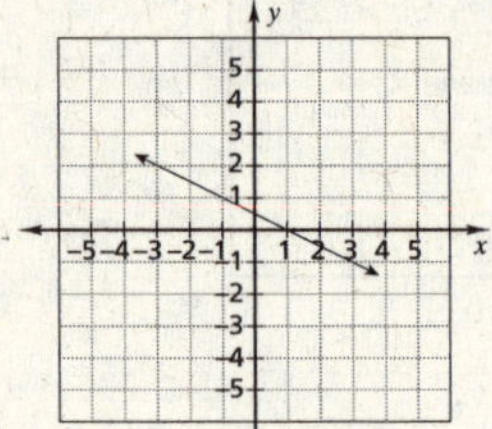

C

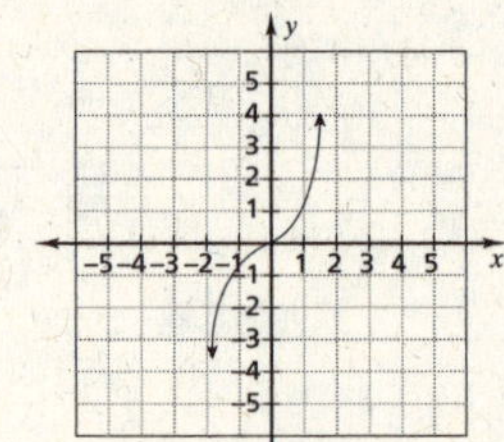

D

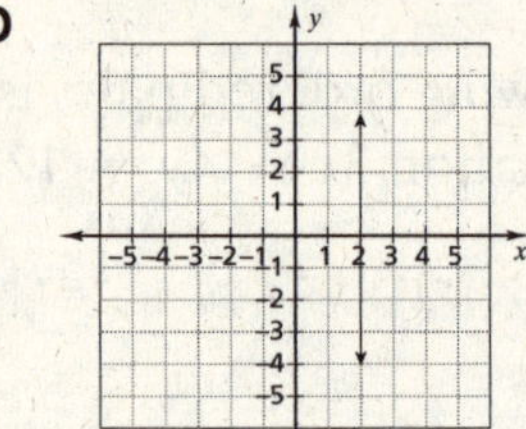

E

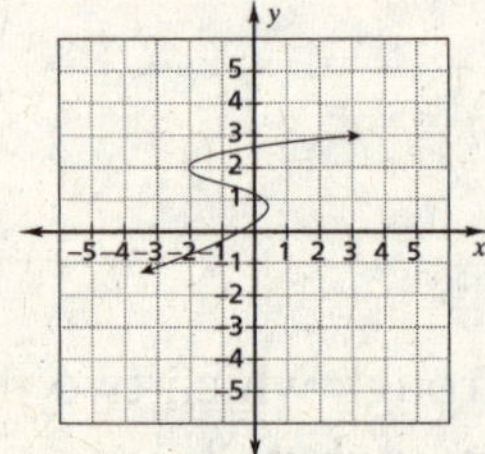

60. What type of trend would you expect to see in a scatter plot comparing a person's height and eye color?

A positive

B negative

C opposite

D none

E inverse

61. You are conducting a survey on a new school color. Which method will give you a random sample?

A Survey all students whose name you pull out of a hat.

B Survey all students who drive a red or blue car.

C Survey all students with a grade point average of 3.5 or better.

D Survey all eighth grade cheerleaders.

E Survey the teachers in the teacher's lounge.

62. A bottle contains 6 red marbles, 9 blue marbles, 3 green marbles, 8 yellow marbles, and 4 white marbles. Which event has the greatest probability?

A *P*(choosing a blue marble)

B *P*(choosing a red or green marble)

C *P*(choosing a yellow or blue marble)

D *P*(choosing a white or green marble)

E *P*(choosing a red or white marble)

63. Ray rolled a number cube 10 times and got the following numbers, 2, 2, 3, 3, 1, 5, 6, 6, 6, 2. What is the difference between the experimental probability of rolling a 6 and the theoretical probability of rolling a 6?

A $\frac{1}{10}$

B $\frac{1}{6}$

C $\frac{2}{15}$

D $\frac{3}{10}$

E $\frac{1}{2}$

GO ON

Name ______________________ Class ______________ Date ______________

Short Constructed Response

64. Describe two ways to find the 15th term of the sequence shown below. Which of these ways would be easier to use if you were to find the 100th term of the sequence? Explain your reasoning.

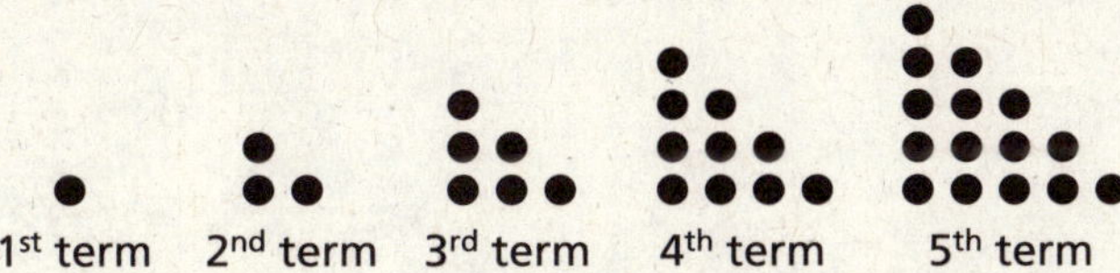

65. Mary planned to spend 20 minutes on the treadmill today at the gym. She spent 5 minutes warming up by walking and then 2 minutes increasing her rate constantly until she was at a full run. She then ran for 6 minutes. At this point the electricity turned off and Mary had to stop instantly. Create a graph that shows how Mary's rate changed throughout the time she was on the treadmill. Explain your reasoning.

66. The president of a sugar company has to choose the least expensive of three different containers in which to package 1,000 cubic centimeters of sugar. It costs $0.50 per square centimeter to make any of the three containers shown below. Which container should the president choose? Why?

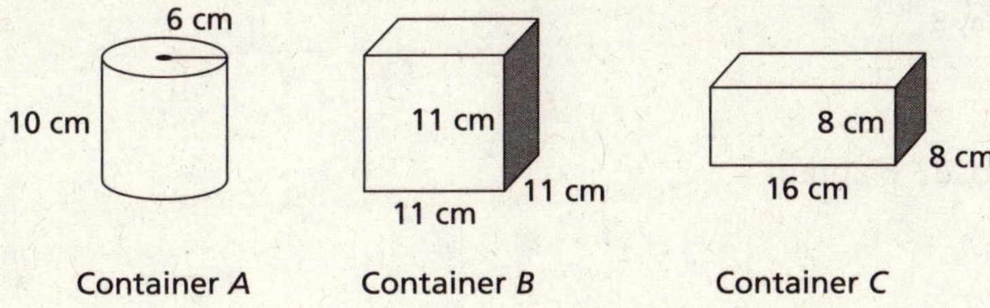

GO ON

Extended Constructed Response

67. You want to enclose a garden in your backyard with segments of fence that are all the same length. The dimensions of the garden are shown below.

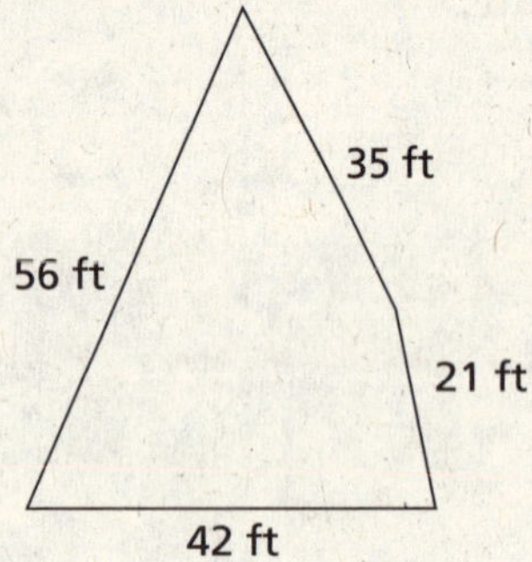

What is the greatest length that a segment of fence can be so that the segments will fill each side without gaps?

If you use segments with the length you found above, how many segments are needed to enclose the entire garden?

68. Every student in the school had three days to vote for their favorite school mascot. The school newspaper published the following bar graph to show how many students liked each of the four different school mascots.

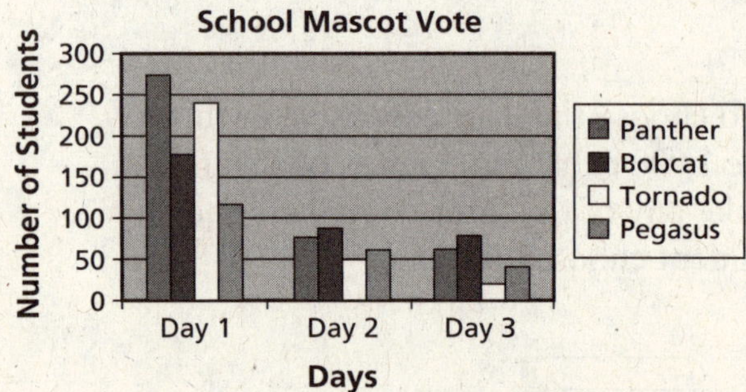

Which mascot should the school choose? Explain.

69. Janell knows that $x < y$ and that $x > 0$ and $y > 0$. She claims that this means that $x^2 < y^2$. Is she correct? Why or why not?

70. Peter travels 90 miles due north and then 60 miles due east to arrive at his grandmother's house. His car gets 25 miles per gallon and he pays $1.12 per gallon of gasoline. Make a diagram of the route Peter travels to his grandmother's house. On your diagram, draw the shortest possible route. If Peter could use the shortest possible route, how much money would he save on gasoline? Explain your answer.

Name ______________________ Class ______________ Date ______________

SAT 10 Practice Test

PS *Mathematics: Problem Solving*

Read each question. Then mark your answer on the answer sheet.

1. Which of these numbers is the coordinate of point Q?

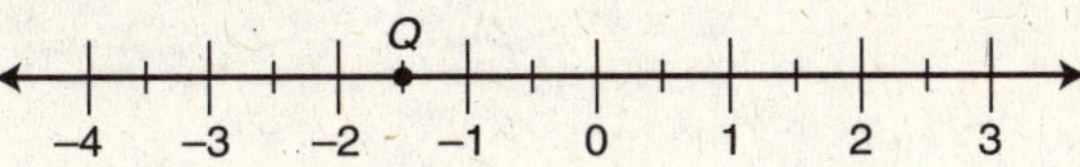

A $\frac{1}{2}$

B $-\frac{1}{2}$

C $-1\frac{1}{2}$

D $-1\frac{3}{4}$

2. Which of these is less than −1.85 but greater than −2?

F −1.9

G −1.8

H $-1\frac{1}{2}$

J 1.7

3. A jeweler sells gold chains that are $\frac{3}{16}$ in., $\frac{1}{8}$ in., $\frac{2}{4}$ in., and $\frac{5}{8}$ in. thick. Which of the following shows these sizes in correct order from smallest to largest?

A $\frac{2}{4}$ in., $\frac{1}{8}$ in., $\frac{5}{8}$ in., $\frac{3}{16}$ in.

B $\frac{1}{4}$ in., $\frac{3}{16}$ in., $\frac{2}{4}$ in., $\frac{5}{8}$ in.

C $\frac{3}{16}$ in., $\frac{1}{8}$ in., $\frac{5}{8}$ in., $\frac{2}{4}$ in.

D $\frac{1}{8}$ in., $\frac{3}{16}$ in., $\frac{2}{4}$ in., $\frac{5}{8}$ in.

4. Odetta found the inside diameter of a tube. She measured the diameter as 0.125 in. What is another way of expressing the length of the diameter?

F $\frac{1}{125}$ in.

G $\frac{1}{12}$ in.

H $\frac{1}{8}$ in.

J $\frac{1}{4}$ in.

5. Which fraction is equivalent to $\frac{36}{45}$ and in lowest terms?

A $\frac{4}{9}$

B $\frac{12}{15}$

C $\frac{4}{5}$

D $\frac{11}{5}$

6. Which of these does NOT have the same value as $1\frac{2}{5}$?

F 1.4

G $\frac{7}{5}$

H 1.40

J 1.25

GO ON

7. **Which of these is a factor of 1,055?**

A 75

B 105

C 201

D 211

8. **Janine knows the area of the base of a prism is 19 yd^2. The height of the prism is 20.8 yd. Which of the following is the best estimate of the capacity of the prism?**

F 200 yd^3

G 300 yd^3

H 350 yd^3

J 400 yd^3

9. **The area of a circle with a radius of 2.6 cm is about 21.2264 cm^2. To which place value is the area expressed?**

A Hundred thousandths

B Ten thousandths

C Thousandths

D Hundredths

10. **The mean distance of the sun from Earth is 1.5 × 10^8 kilometers. Which of the following shows the number in standard from?**

F 15,000,000

G 150,000,000

H 1,500,000,000

J 15,000,000,000

11. **Which is the solution of $3x + 4 = -11$?**

A $x = -45$

B $x = -15$

C $x = -5$

D $x = -2\frac{1}{3}$

12. **Which expression is equivalent to $4 \times 5\frac{1}{2}$?**

F $4\left(5 + \frac{1}{2}\right)$

G $20\frac{1}{2}$

H $4\left(5 \times \frac{1}{2}\right)$

J $4 + \left(5 \times \frac{1}{2}\right)$

13. **Mr. Herold repairs dishwashers. He charges $25 for a house call that is more than 30 miles from his shop plus $20 per hour. If *h* represents the hours he must work on a machine 45 miles from his shop, which of the following expressions could be used to find his fee?**

A $20h$

B $25h + 20$

C $20h + 25$

D $60h$

GO ON

PS SAT 10 Practice Test

14. **What is the value of $4a + 2a - b$ if $a = 3$ and $b = 4$?**

F 9

G 10

H 14

J 17

15. **This graph shows the Ramirez family budget. Which expenses together make up less than 25% of the budget?**

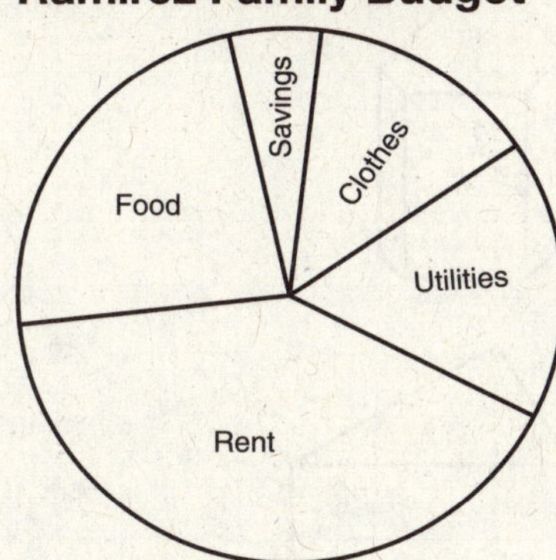

A Savings and rent

B Savings and clothes

C Food and rent

D Food and clothes

16. **Find the missing output value for this table.**

Input	1	2	10	5
Output	5	9	41	?

F 10

G 12

H 20

J 21

17. **What is the tenth term in the pattern given below?**

−1, 1, 3, 5, . . .

A 17

B 16

C 15

D 14

18. **A recipe for fruit punch mixes 2 L of orange juice, 3 L of pineapple juice, and 1 L of seltzer. How many liters of orange juice will be needed if 18 L of pineapple juice are used?**

F 18 L

G 12 L

H 9 L

J 6 L

19. **The results of a survey showed that 80% of the people surveyed planned to vote for the town referendum to improve the town's street lights. If 200 people were part of the survey, how many were planning to vote for this improvement?**

A 40 people

B 160 people

C 180 people

D 200 people

GO ON

20. A letter is chosen at random from the word MISSISSIPPI. What is the probability that the chosen letter is an S?

F $\frac{1}{11}$

G $\frac{1}{4}$

H $\frac{4}{11}$

J $\frac{4}{7}$

21. Classify $\angle BEC$.

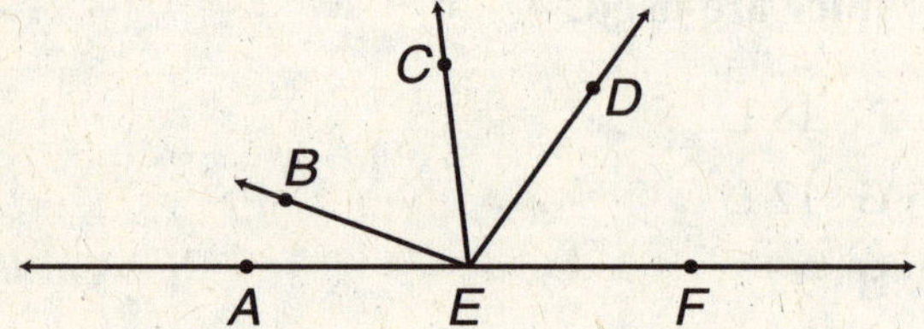

A Straight

B Obtuse

C Right

D Acute

22. Luke wants to classify these polyhedrons. Which polyhedron is not a prism?

F
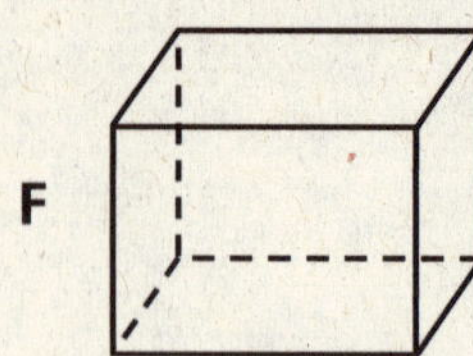

G

H
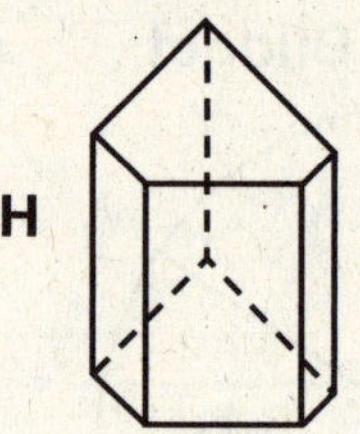

J
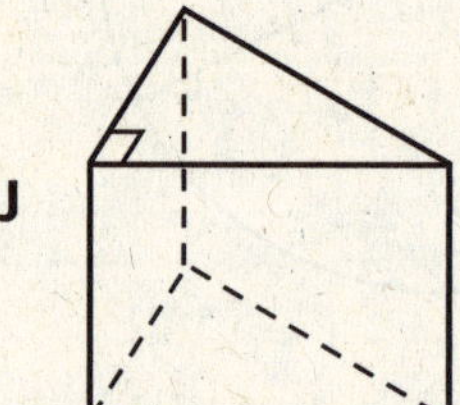

GO ON

Name ______________________ Class ______________ Date ______________

PS SAT 10 Practice Test

23. This line graph shows the temperature in the lobby and on the 15th floor of an office building during several different times of the day. What is the greatest difference between the temperatures in the two floors at any given time?

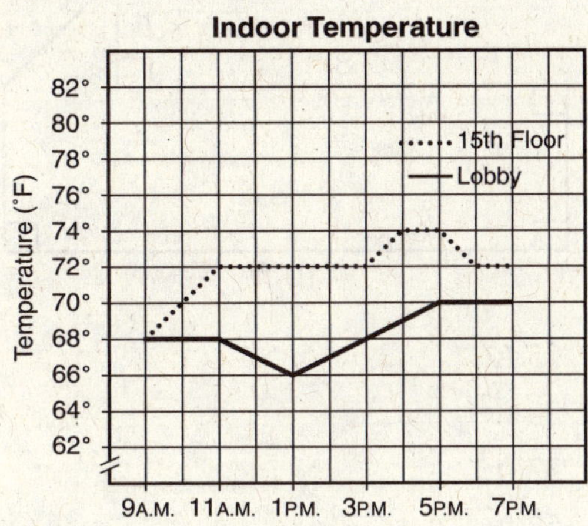

A 10°F

B 8°F

C 6°F

D 4°F

24. This table shows the amount of cereal that is packed into small boxes of granola.

Boxes of Cereal	Number of Grams (g)
1	400 g
2	800 g
3	1200 g
4	1600 g

If this pattern continues, how many grams of cereal would there be in 9 boxes?

F 3000 g

G 3200 g

H 3600 g

J 4200 g

25. Maurice recorded the number of hours he worked in each of the past five weeks: 32.5, 40.5, 37.75, 20.0, and 31.5. What is the mean number of hours per week worked over the five-week period?

A 30.75 hours

B 32.45 hours

C 32.6 hours

D 33 hours

26. This chart shows the results of spinning a blue, red, and white spinner.

Spins	Tally
Blue	𝍸 𝍸
Red	𝍸 𝍸 IIII
White	II

How many spins were there in all?

F 10 spins

G 22 spins

H 24 spins

J 26 spins

27. Tyrone has seven books on his desk between bookends. In how many different ways can he arrange the books from left to right?

A 14 ways

B 49 ways

C 720 ways

D 5040 ways

GO ON

28. Which of the following is a radius of circle O?

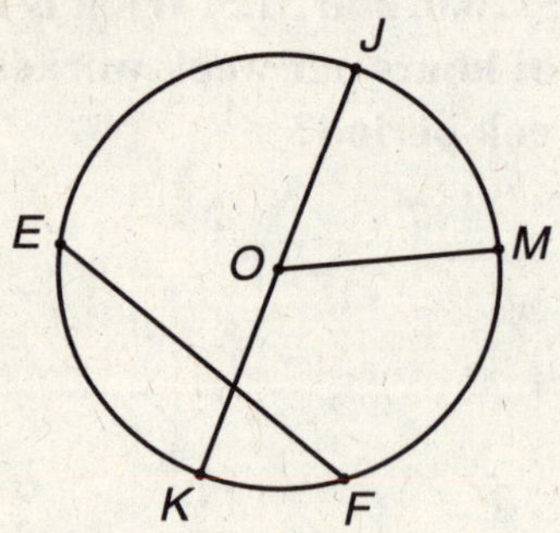

F O

G $\overline{OM}$

H $\overline{EF}$

J $\overline{JK}$

29. Use the figure.

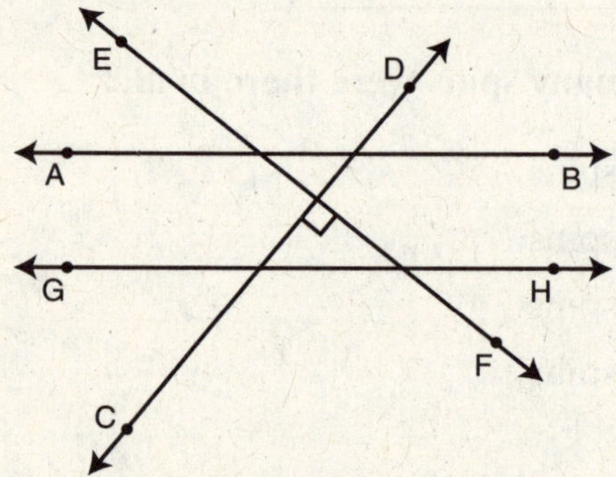

Which of these is true?

A $\overleftrightarrow{AB}$ and $\overleftrightarrow{CD}$ are perpendicular.

B $\overleftrightarrow{EF}$ and $\overleftrightarrow{AB}$ are perpendicular.

C $\overleftrightarrow{CD}$ and $\overleftrightarrow{EF}$ are perpendicular.

D $\overleftrightarrow{GH}$ and $\overleftrightarrow{AB}$ are perpendicular.

30. John wants a garden that is at least 64 square feet. His friend sketched a garden design as shown below. How many more square feet does the garden have to be in order to meet John's area requirements?

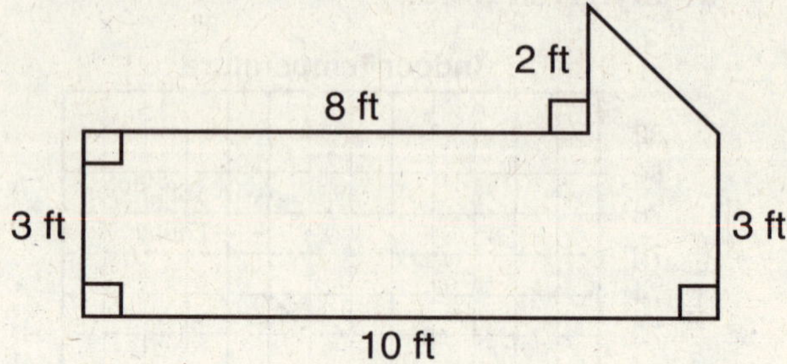

F 25 ft^2

G 30 ft^2

H 32 ft^2

J 52 ft^2

31. To the nearest hundredth, what is the circumference of the circle?

Use $C = \pi d$ and $\pi \approx 3.14$.

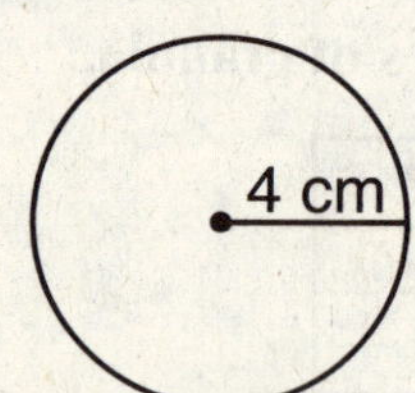

A 12.56 cm

B 25.12 cm

C 50.24 cm

D 97.21 cm

GO ON

Name ______________________ Class ______________ Date ______________

PS SAT 10 Practice Test

32. The aquarium is a rectangular prism with dimensions 30 in. by 20 in. by 16 in. Estimate the maximum volume of water it can hold.

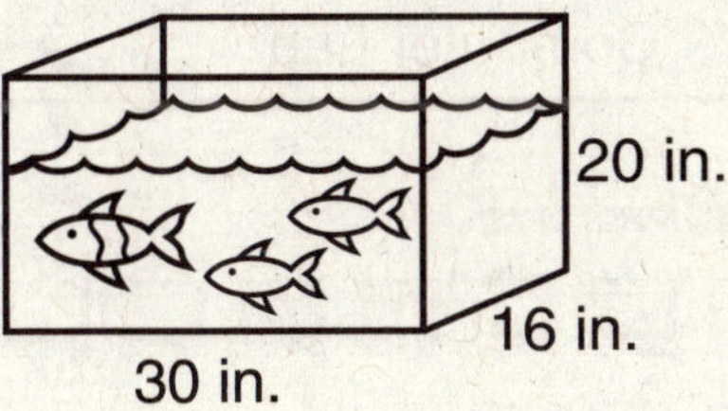

F 960 in^3

G 4800 in^3

H 9000 in^3

J $18{,}000 \text{ in}^3$

33. Triangle *ABC* is moved to form triangle *A′B′C′*. What is the best description of this transformation?

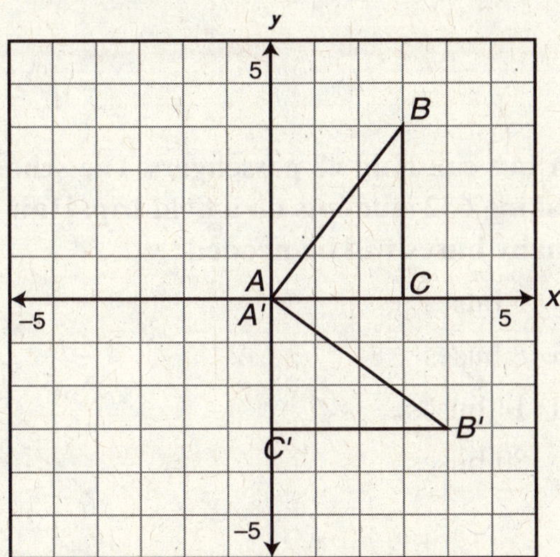

A A translation 4 units down

B A reflection across the x-axis

C A clockwise rotation of 90°

D A clockwish rotation of 180°

34. Triangle *ABC* is a right triangle. The coordinates of *A* are (−2, 1) and the coordinates of *B* are (3, 1). Which of the following could be the coordinates of *C*?

F $(3, 5)$

G $(5, -1)$

H $(2, 4)$

J $(-1, 3)$

35. A cable is 78 m long. Workers cut it into 30 pieces of equal length. How many millimeters long is each piece?

A 26 mm

B 260 mm

C 2600 mm

D 26,000 mm

36. Use the centimeter ruler. Find the perimeter of rectangle *PQRS*.

F 10 cm

G 20 cm

H 24 cm

J 40 cm

GO ON

37. Ralph left home at 7:25 A.M. He returned home at 9:08 P.M. What was the elapsed time?

A 1 hr 43 min

B 13 hr 43 min

C 13 hr 83 min

D 14 hr 23 min

38. Triangle *ABC* is similar to triangle *DEF*. Find the length of *x*.

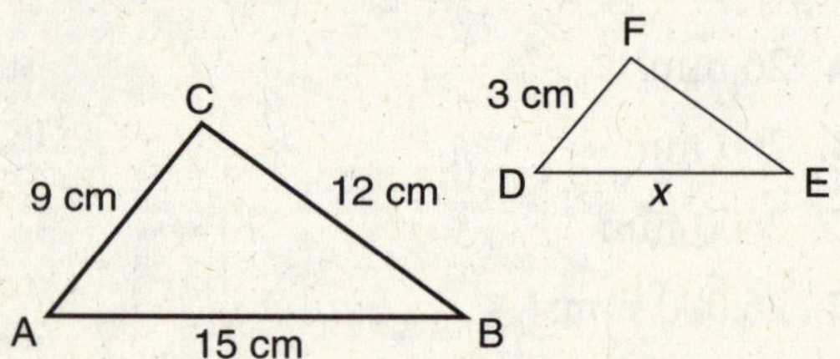

F 3 cm

G 4 cm

H 5 cm

J 6 cm

39. A scale drawing shows the plan for a computer lab. The length of the longest wall on the drawing is $3\frac{1}{4}$ in. What is the actual length of the wall in feet?

$\frac{1}{4}$ in. = 2 ft

A 8 ft

B 24 cm

C 26 ft

D 28 ft

40. A bus can hold 48 passengers. The school is taking 632 students on a field trip. How many buses will be needed?

F 5 buses

G 8 buses

H 14 buses

J 80 buses

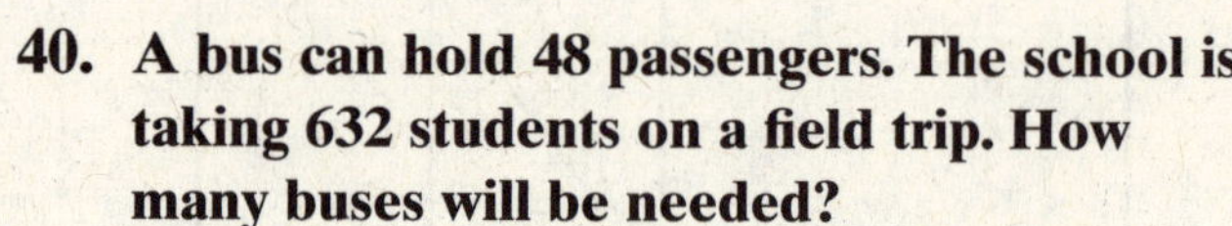

GO ON

PS SAT 10 Practice Test

41. Alice is remodeling her home. She has remodeling bills for the following amounts: $834, $792, $810, and $795. Which of these is the best estimate of the cost of her remodeling?

A $2800

B $3200

C $4000

D $4800

42. Which of these is the best estimate of the area of the figure below?

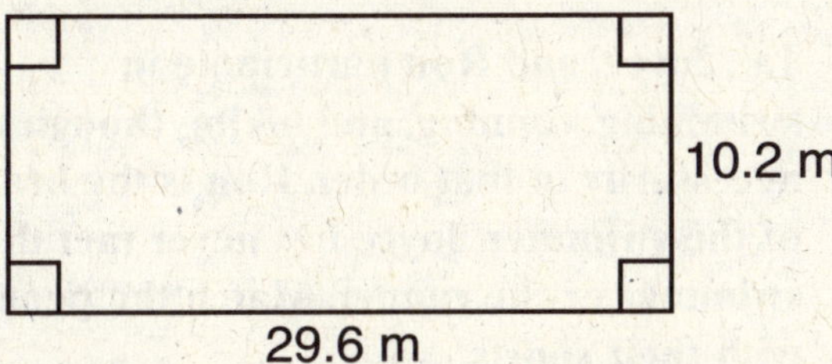

F 270 m^2

G 279 m2

H 300 m^2

J 310 m^2

43. Tamara received a 5% wage increase. She earns $198 a week. Estimate how much of a weekly wage increase she received.

A $5

B $10

C $20

D $100

44. Darrel finds two pieces of wire that measure $\frac{7}{12}$ in. and $\frac{7}{8}$ in. Estimate the total length of the two pieces of wire together.

F $\frac{1}{2}$ in.

G 1 in.

H $1\frac{1}{2}$ in.

J 2 in.

45. Liz is buying tubes of oil paint at an art supply store. Each tube of paint costs between $2 and $3. What is a reasonable cost for 12 tubes of paint?

A $20

B $30

C $38

D $40

GO ON

46. This table lists the cost of tickets to the state fair. On Saturday, 503 tickets were sold. What information do you need to find out how much money was collected on Saturday?

State Fair Tickets	
Adult	$8
Child	$3

F The price of a ticket

G The number of tickets sold on Sunday

H The number of adult tickets sold on Saturday

J The number of senior citizens who attended on Saturday

47. Jan opened a box of computer disks. She gave half of the disks to her brother. She gave her friend Lisa 5 disks. She put 10 disks in her school bag. Then Jan had 5 disks left in the box. How many disks were in the box when she first opened it?

A 40 disks

B 30 disks

C 20 disks

D 10 disks

48. Keri studied for 95 minutes. She studied math 6 minutes longer than she studied science. She studied history 8 minutes longer than she studied math. How long did she study science?

F 20 minutes

G 25 minutes

H 30 minutes

J 35 minutes

49. A community center uses a phone tree to tell members important information. The center leader makes 2 calls to start the phone tree. Then each person who gets a call makes 2 calls. So on the second round, 4 calls are made. On the third round 8 calls are made. How many calls are made on the fifth round?

A 32 calls

B 24 calls

C 16 calls

D 12 calls

50. Tai, Joyce, and Ron participate in swimming, running, and hiking though not necessarily in that order. Ron is the brother of the swimmer. Joyce has never met the swimmer or the runner. Match the people with their sports.

F Tai is the runner, Joyce is the swimmer, and Ron is the hiker.

G Tai is the hiker, Joyce is the runner, and Ron is the swimmer.

H Tai is the runner, Joyce is the hiker, and Ron is the swimmer.

J Tai is the swimmer, Joyce is the hiker, and Ron is the runner.

Name ______________________ Class ______________ Date ______________

SAT 10 Practice Test

Mathematics: Procedures

Find each answer. Then mark the space on your answer sheet. If a correct answer is not here, mark the space for NH.

1. $\begin{array}{r} 39 \\ \times\ 34 \\ \hline \end{array}$

A 1126

B 1296

C 1316

D 1446

E NH

2. $\begin{array}{r} 740 \\ \times\ 29 \\ \hline \end{array}$

F 20,460

G 21,460

H 22,360

J 22,870

K NH

3. $25\overline{)5245}$

A $29\frac{4}{5}$

B $209\frac{4}{5}$

C $290\frac{4}{5}$

D $299\frac{4}{5}$

E NH

4. $12.23 \times 0.4 =$

F 489.2

G 48.92

H 4.892

J 0.4892

K NH

5. $1\frac{5}{13} + 3\frac{9}{13} =$

A $4\frac{1}{13}$

B $4\frac{7}{13}$

C $5\frac{1}{13}$

D $5\frac{7}{13}$

E NH

6. $\frac{2}{3} \times \frac{9}{5} =$

F $2\frac{7}{10}$

G $1\frac{3}{5}$

H $1\frac{1}{5}$

J $\frac{10}{27}$

K NH

7. $1.4\overline{)0.84}$

A 60

B 6.0

C 0.6

D 0.06

E NH

GO ON

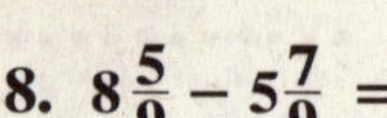

SAT 10 Practice Test

8. $8\frac{5}{9} - 5\frac{7}{9} =$

F $\frac{7}{9}$

G $2\frac{7}{9}$

H $3\frac{2}{9}$

J $3\frac{7}{9}$

K NH

9. The distance from the house to the garage is 120 feet. Telephone wire is sold by the yard. How many yards should Mr. Lewis buy if he wants enough wire to reach from the house to the garage?

A 10 yd

B 40 yd

C 60 yd

D 80 yd

E NH

10. Allie reviewed her company's travel mileage for the past four months. What was the company's total mileage for these months?

Month	Total Mileage
April	17,281
May	5,326
June	42,381
July	2,580

F 66,568 mi

G 67,568 mi

H 67,668 mi

J 68,468 mi

K NH

11. An artist pours 1700 cm^3 of plaster into a mold to make a prism. She has 7000 cm^3 of plaster. How many times can she completely fill the mold?

A 4

B 5

C 30

D 41

E NH

12. Laura and Bert sold tickets to the school play. Each ticket costs $6. Laura sold 7 tickets. Bert sold 5 tickets. How much money in all should Laura and Bert have collected?

F $72

G $42

H $30

J $12

K NH

13. Jamal has the following scores on his math tests: 85, 92, 79, 94, and 100. What is the average (mean) of his test scores?

A 21

B 75

C 90

D 92

E NH

Name ______________________ Class ______________ Date ______________

SAT 10 Practice Test

14. Miko has $2486 in her checking account. She wants to write a check for $3291. How much does she need to deposit before writing the check?

F $705

G $803

H $820

J $825

K NH

15. A rectangular field has a perimeter of 13.34 km. The width of the field is 2.17 km. What is the length of the field?

A 11.17 km

B 9 km

C 4.5 km

D 2.25 km

E NH

16. This year 4% of the people in a village do not have a television set. If 250 people do not have a television set, how many people live in the village?

F 6250 people

G 1000 people

H 62.5 people

J 31 people

K NH

17. Samantha bought three magazines for $2.95 each and two cards for $1.86 each. How much did she spend?

A $23.68

B $12.47

C $11.57

D $10.68

E NH

18. At the EZ Market, apples are usually $1.29 lb. This week they are on sale for $0.99 lb. How much will Ms. Sanchez save if she buys 5 pounds of apples this week?

F $0.30

G $1.50

H $4.95

J $5.19

K NH

19.

Port St. Lucie, Florida	Population
2000	89,000
1990	55,761
1980	14,690

How many more people lived in Port St. Lucie in 1990 than in 1980?

A 70,451 people

B 41,071 people

C 39,280 people

D 30,690 people

E NH

20. Mr. Lammers bought $4\frac{3}{4}$ yd of felt at $4 per yd. How much did he spend on felt in all?

F $16.75

G $19.00

H $20.00

J $28.00

K NH

21. A bolt of fabric contains 30 yards of material. How much material remains on the bolt once you cut off a $5\frac{1}{4}$-yard piece of fabric?

A $1\frac{2}{4}$ yd

B $5\frac{1}{4}$ yd

C $24\frac{3}{4}$ yd

D $26\frac{3}{4}$ yd

E NH

22. Jeremy had 10.33 yards of flannel. He used 9.66 yd of flannel to make holiday decorations. How much flannel does he have left?

F 0.33 yd

G 0.50 yd

H 0.67 yd

J 1 yd

K NH

23. The directions said to travel $\frac{3}{10}$ mi from the highway to the town square, then travel $\frac{3}{5}$ mi on Route 15 to Tom's house. What is the total distance in miles from the highway to Tom's house?

A $\frac{9}{10}$ mi

B $\frac{4}{5}$ mi

C $\frac{7}{10}$ mi

D $\frac{1}{2}$ mi

E NH

24. A room measures $14\frac{1}{2}$ ft by 20 ft. Find the area of the room in square feet using the formula $A = l \times w$.

F 140 ft^2

G 200 ft^2

H 290 ft^2

J 330 ft^2

K NH

25. A tile setter is tiling a floor with tiles that measure $\frac{2}{3}$ ft on each side. If he uses 19 tiles along the wall, how long is the wall?

A $12\frac{1}{3}$ ft

B $12\frac{2}{3}$ ft

C $13\frac{1}{3}$ ft

D $13\frac{2}{3}$ ft

E NH

GO ON

SAT 10 Practice Test

26. Jei's cousin can walk about $\frac{3}{4}$ mile per hour.

At that rate, how many miles can she walk in 3 hours?

F $\frac{7}{8}$ mi

G $1\frac{1}{2}$ mi

H $2\frac{1}{4}$ mi

J $3\frac{1}{4}$ mi

K NH

27. Sarah picked a $5\frac{3}{4}$-pound pumpkin on Monday and a $3\frac{3}{8}$-pound pumpkin on Saturday.

$5\frac{3}{4}$ lb  **$3\frac{3}{8}$ lb** 

How many pounds did both pumpkins weigh all together?

A $5\frac{1}{2}$ lb

B $6\frac{1}{4}$ lb

C $8\frac{1}{8}$ lb

D $9\frac{1}{8}$ lb

E NH

28. Jason traveled 14.593 miles. Alyce traveled 29.193 miles. How many more miles did Alyce travel than Jason?

F 14.5

G 14.59

H 14.6

J 14.9

K NH

29. Myra bought these jeans for $10 off the price shown.

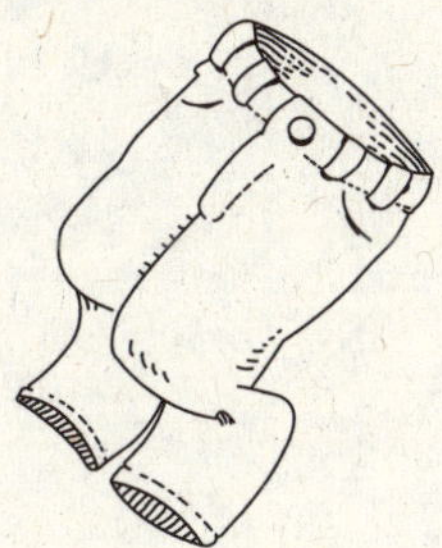

What percent discount did she receive?

A 10%

B 20%

C 25%

D 30%

E NH

30. This oil drum was stored in Lila's garage.

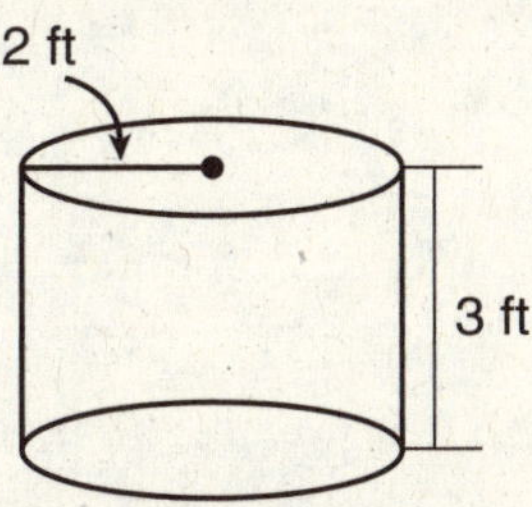

Lila calculated the volume of the oil drum to be about 37.68 ft^3. If the drum is 90% full, what is the current capacity of the drum?

F 3.768 ft^3

G 18.840 ft^3

H 33.842 ft^3

J 33.912 ft^3

K NH

Name ____________ Class ____________ Date ____________

ITBS Practice Test

Read each question and choose the best answer. Then mark the space on the answer sheet for the answer you have chosen.

1. **Anastasia was reviewing her company's travel mileage for the past four months. She recorded 42,381; 2580; 17,281; and 5326 miles. What was her company's total mileage for these months?**

   A 67,568 mi

   B 67,668 mi

   C 66,568 mi

   D 67,567 mi

2. **Miko had $2486 in her bank account last week. She then wanted to write a check for $3291. How much does she need to deposit before writing the check?**

   F $805

   G $705

   H $820

   J $740

3. **Marilyn got a loan to buy a new car. The monthly payment is $328.70. She has to make payments for five years. What is the total she will pay for the car?**

   A $19,822

   B $19,722

   C over $20,000

   D less than $15,000

4. **The navigation team for a planned spaceflight calculated that it will take 25 years to travel 4.2 light years. How many light years will the spacecraft cover each year?**

   F 0.168 light year

   G 105 light years

   H 0.16 light year

   J 5.95 light years

5. **Simplify $\frac{5}{12} + \frac{7}{20}$.**

   A $\frac{12}{240}$

   B $\frac{48}{60}$

   C $\frac{23}{30}$

   D $\frac{23}{20}$

6. **Simplify $\frac{13}{18} - \frac{7}{12}$.**

   F 1

   G $\frac{6}{6}$

   H $\frac{5}{36}$

   J $\frac{6}{36}$

GO ON

ITBS Practice Test

7. Multiply $\frac{3}{8} \times \frac{1}{7}$.

A $\frac{24}{56}$

B $\frac{4}{15}$

C $\frac{8}{21}$

D $\frac{3}{56}$

8. What is the quotient when you divide $\frac{2}{3}$ by $\frac{5}{9}$?

F $2\frac{7}{10}$

G $\frac{10}{27}$

H $1\frac{3}{5}$

J $1\frac{1}{5}$

9. Find the sum: 2.013 + 28.7 + 7.21.

A 3.792

B 30.3309

C 12.093

D 37.923

10. When you subtract 6.3 from 12.027, how many digits are there to the right of the decimal point in the answer?

F 0

G 1

H 0

J 3

11. Which statement is true of the following problem?

21.62 × 3.08

A You must line up the decimal points before multiplying.

B The answer has two digits to the right of the decimal point.

C The answer is less than 67.

D The answer is more than 68.

12. A rectangular field has an area of 26.04 km^2. Two sides are each 12 km long. What is the length of each of the other two sides?

F 312. 48 km

G 2.17 km

H 12 km

J 24 km

GO ON

Name ______________________ Class ______________ Date ______________

ITBS Practice Test

13. Which of these is NOT true of the answer to the problem?

47.3193 ÷ 2.08

A It has more than four digits to the right of the decimal point.

B It can be written as a fraction.

C It is a rational number.

D It is an irrational number.

14. Maryann bought 8 CDs at $8.97 each. What did she pay for all eight?

F $112.12

G $71.76

H $8.97

J More than $72

15. In a relay race, the first runner ran 236 meters. The second runner ran 812 meters. The third runner ran 2007 meters. What was the total distance they ran?

A 1018 meters

B 3055 meters

C 30,550 meters

D 3000 meters

16. Samantha bought three magazines for $2.95 each, and two cards for $1.86 each. How much did she spend?

F $11.57

G $12.57

H $4.81

J $23.68

17. Evaluate the expression.

$$\frac{7}{12}\left(\frac{1}{3}+\frac{3}{4}\right)-\frac{5}{8}$$

A $\frac{1}{144}$

B $\frac{1}{12}$

C $\frac{1}{4}$

D $\frac{4}{144}$

18. Suppose you toss a coin and toss a single die. How many possible outcomes are there?

F 12

G 2

H 8

J 6

GO ON

19. **Which algebraic expression describes the pattern 5, 7, 9, 11, 13, . . . ?**

A $2x + 1$

B $2x + 3$

C add 10 each time

D add 2 to the tens digit each time

20. **What is the missing value in the table below?**

1	2	3	4
3	6	9	12
9	18	27	36
27	54	81	

F 72

G 108

H 27

J 48

21. **What are the missing values in the table below?**

n	2	4	6	8
$5n - 4$	6	16		

A 36 and 56

B 36 and 46

C 18 and 36

D 26 and 36

22. **Jason's father drove 486 miles on vacation. The car used 33.3 gallons of fuel. Express the fuel consumption in miles per gallon, to the nearest tenth.**

F 14.3 miles/gallon

G 13.6 miles/gallon

H 14.7 miles/gallon

J 14.6 miles/gallon

23. **Which linear equation best fits the following data points?**

(1, 3.1), (2, 4.8), (3, 6.7), (4, 9.2)

A $y = 2x + 2$

B $y = 3x - 5$

C $y = x + 4$

D $y = 2x + 1$

24. **Which linear equation best fits the following data points?**

(1, 1.2), (4, 9.8), (7, 18.6)

F $y = 3\frac{x}{3}$

G $y = 3x - 1$

H $y = 2x + 5$

J $y = 3x - 2$

GO ON

Name ____________________ Class ______________ Date ______________

ITBS Practice Test

25. Which of these sets of numbers has elements that are all divisible by 3?

A {12, 21, 27, 33}

B {13, 23, 33, 43}

C {21, 27, 19, 63}

D {24, 9, 27, 83}

26. Which algebraic expression best describes the pattern?

3, 8, 13, 18, 23, 28, . . .

F $5x - 2$

G $3x + 7$

H $10x + 3$

J $x^2 - 7$

27. Which figure is NOT a quadrilateral?

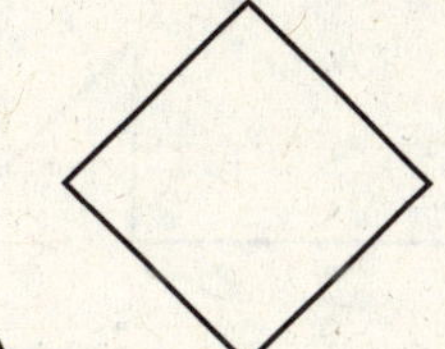

A

B

C

D

GO ON

ITBS Practice Test

28. Which of these is the area of the figure below?

F 32 square units

G 52 square units

H 25 square units

J 30 square units

29. Which of these is the best estimate of the area of the figure below?

A 279 m^2

B 300 m^2

C 270 m^2

D 310 m^2

30. Of the numbers $\frac{4}{7}$, $\frac{7}{9}$, $\frac{8}{10}$, 0.71, and 0.59, which is the greatest?

F $\frac{7}{9}$

G $\frac{8}{10}$

H 0.71

J $\frac{4}{7}$

31. An employee of a large company was paid $48.75 for working 7.5 hours. What was the employee's rate of pay?

A $6.50/hour

B $6.25/hour

C $6.75/hour

D $7.50/hour

32. Larry recorded the number of hours he worked in each of the past five weeks; 32.6, 40.7, 37.4, 20.8, and 31.4. What is the mean number of hours per week worked over the five-week period?

F 32.6 hours

G 30.75 hours

H 32.58 hours

J 33 hours

GO ON

Name ________ Class ________ Date ________

ITBS Practice Test

33. Solve for x.

$$5x - 4 = 8 - x$$

A 0

B 1

C 3

D 2

34. Use rounding to estimate the difference, 13.98 − 7.36.

F 8

G 5

H 6

J 7

35. Round 23.1743 to the hundredths place.

A 23.174

B 23.2

C 23.18

D 23.17

36. Which of the following would you estimate to be $1\frac{1}{2}$?

F $\frac{4}{7} + \frac{8}{9}$

G $\frac{6}{7} + \frac{4}{5}$

H $\frac{8}{9} + \frac{11}{12}$

J $\frac{1}{7} + \frac{5}{7}$

37. Which of the following would you estimate to be 0?

A $\frac{4}{7} - \frac{5}{8}$

B $\frac{8}{9} - \frac{1}{3}$

C $\frac{12}{11} - \frac{1}{4}$

D $\frac{5}{6} - \frac{1}{8}$

GO ON

ITBS Practice Test

38. Which is the best estimate for the length of the side labeled *x*?

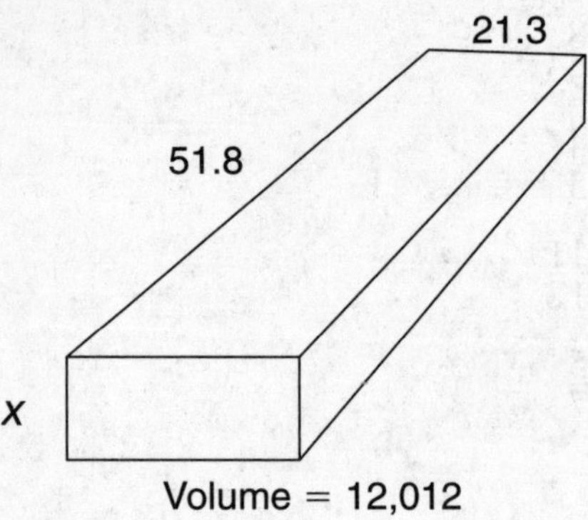

F 8

G 12

H 13

J 16

39. Which of these is an underestimate of the sum of 21.4, 30.8, 7.4, and 16.3?

A 77

B 78

C 76

D 74

40. Which of these is the best estimate of the sum?

$$\begin{array}{r} 83.4 \\ 16.8 \\ 7.3 \\ +\ 12.4 \\ \hline \end{array}$$

F 108

G 119

H 130

J 1,199

Name ______________________ Class ______________ Date ______________

TerraNova Practice Test

Part 1

Read each question and choose the best answer. Then mark the space on the answer sheet for the answer you have chosen.

1 $\frac{3}{8} + \frac{1}{6} =$

A $\frac{27}{48}$

B $\frac{13}{24}$

C $\frac{2}{7}$

D $\frac{1}{6}$

E None of these

2 $\frac{1}{2} \times \frac{2}{3} =$

F $\frac{1}{3}$

G $\frac{2}{5}$

H $\frac{1}{6}$

J $\frac{1}{2}$

3 $-96 + (-12) =$

A -84

B 84

C -108

D 108

E None of these

4 $0.4\overline{)10.16}$

F 0.0254

G 0.254

H 2.54

J 25.4

K None of these

5 85% of 32 =

A 272

B 37.6

C 27.2

D 0.272

E None of these

6 $8 \div 11 =$

F 0.72

G 0.727

H $0.\overline{72}$

J $0.\overline{727}$

K None of these

7 $2(10 - 8) + 8 \div 4 =$

A 14

B 6

C 5

D 3

E None of these

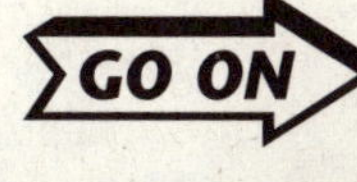

8 Which is the name of this polyhedron?

F Triangular pyramid

G Rectangular pyramid

H Hexagonal pyramid

J Octagonal pyramid

9 A fish tank is a rectangular prism with dimensions 30 inches by 20 inches by 16 inches. What is the maximum volume of water it can hold?

A 480 in^3

B 960 in^3

C 4,800 in^3

D 9,600 in^3

10 Which addition problem does the model represent?

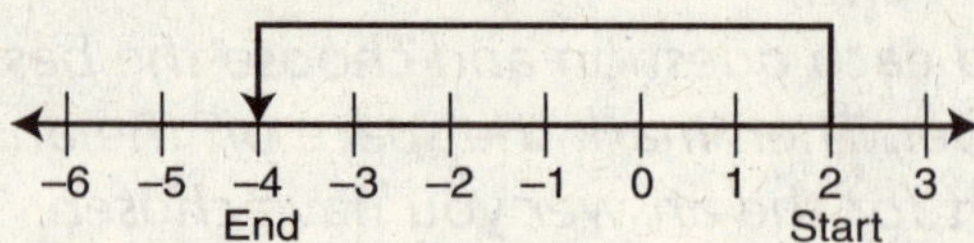

F $2 + (-4) = -2$

G $-4 + (-6) = -10$

H $-4 + (-4) = -8$

J $2 + (-6) = -4$

11 What number can go in the box to make the sentence true?

$(\square - 6) \div 5 = 30$

A 150

B 156

C 144

D 12

12 Which fraction forms a terminating decimal?

F $\frac{6}{11}$

G $\frac{4}{9}$

H $\frac{3}{5}$

J $\frac{5}{12}$

GO ON

Name ______________________ Class ______________ Date ______________

TerraNova Practice Test

13 **Find the ratio of the number of shaded squares to the total number of squares.**

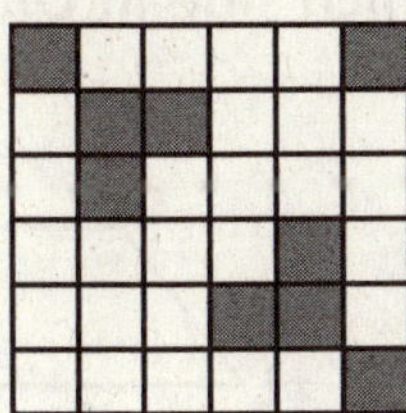

A $\frac{1}{4}$

B $\frac{1}{3}$

C $\frac{3}{1}$

D $\frac{4}{1}$

14 **A 10-foot ladder leans against a building with the base of the ladder 6 feet from the building. How high is the point where the ladder touches the building?**

F 9 ft

G 8 ft

H 7 ft

J 6 ft

15 **Which fraction, percent, or decimal does the shaded area represent?**

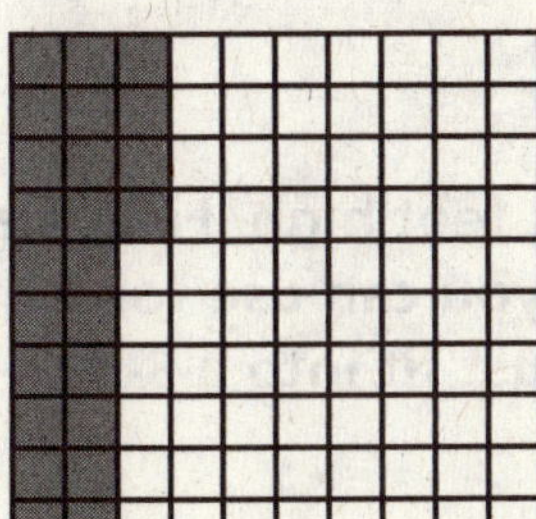

A 24%

B $\frac{24}{10}$

C 2.4

D $\frac{24}{100}\%$

16 **Ken and Lu decide to keep a bar graph showing how many books each of them read for four months. In which month was the total books read the greatest?**

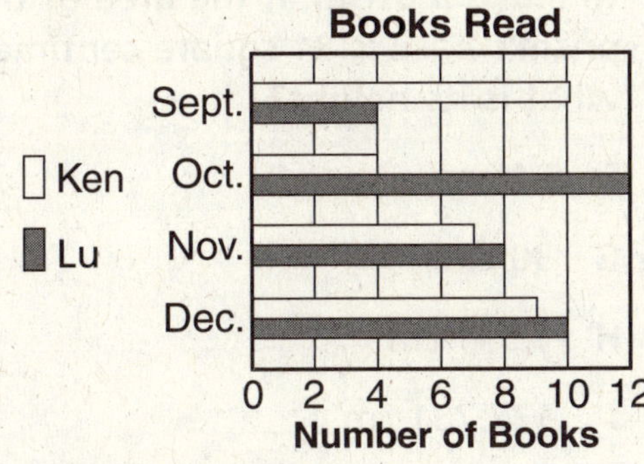

F September

G October

H November

J December

17 **Tsao Lin is evaluating shoe box racks for use in a shoe manufacturing plant. The number of boxes in the rack must be divisible by both 6 and 8. Which of the following rack capacities can she use?**

A 112

B 184

C 192

D 204

STOP

TerraNova Practice Test

Part 2

18 **An artist pours 1,701 cubic centimeters of plaster into a mold to make a prism. If the area of the prism's base is 81 square centimeters, what is its height?**

F 21 cm

G 30 cm

H 1,541 cm

J 137,781 cm

19 **How do you find the volume of a cylinder?**

A Multiply the base circumference times the height.

B Multiply $\frac{1}{2}$ the base circumference times the height.

C Multiply the base area times the height.

D Multiply $\frac{1}{2}$ the base area times the height.

20 **Use the formula $c = \frac{f}{8}$ to change fluid ounces (f) into cups (c). How many cups are equal to 48 fluid ounces?**

F 4 cups

G 6 cups

H 8 cups

J 10 cups

21 ***QRST* ~ *JKLM*. Which side in *QRST* corresponds to $\overline{JK}$?**

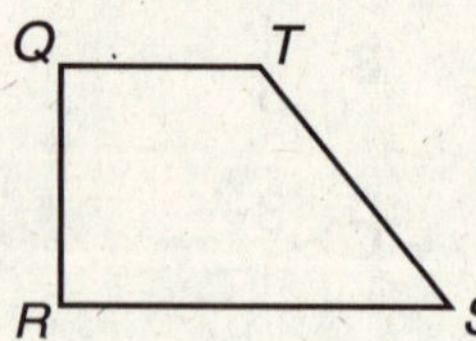

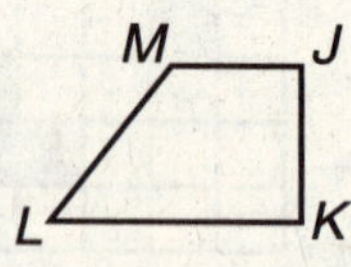

A $\overline{QT}$

B $\overline{QR}$

C $\overline{RS}$

D $\overline{TS}$

22 **$\triangle ABC \sim \triangle DEF$. Find x.**

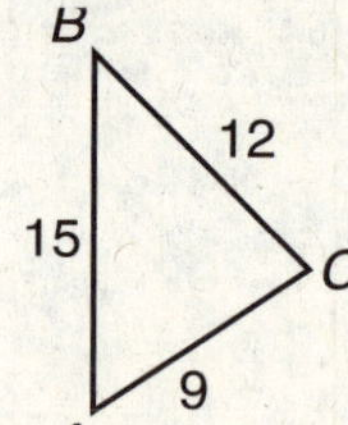

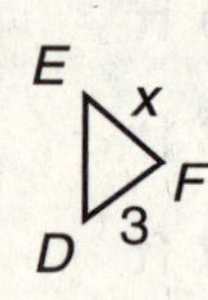

F $x = 6$

G $x = 5$

H $x = 4$

J $x = 3$

23 **A statue is 12 feet high. Find the largest scale you can use for a model statue if it must fit into a 3-inch-high box.**

A 1 in.:4 ft

B 1 in.:3 ft

C 3 in.:1 ft

D 4 in.:1 ft

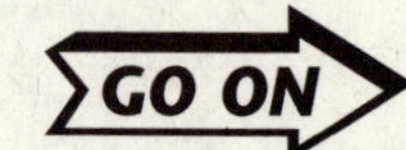

TerraNova Practice Test

24 **Which expression would give you the best estimate of 49% of 377?**

F 49% of 300

G 49% of 350

H 50% of 350

J 50% of 380

25 **Mike mows lawns. He charges $3.50 per lawn. Mike earned $21.00 this week. How many lawns did he mow?**

A 8

B 7

C 6

D 5

26 **Melora volunteers at the library every 14th day and at the hospital every 12th day. On which day will she volunteer at both the library and the hospital?**

F Day 96

G Day 72

H Day 84

J Day 108

27 **As shown in the table, the cost of renting a video camera depends on the number of days you rent it. Which equation represents the relationship between cost and number of days?**

Days	2	4	5	7
Cost ($)	12	24	30	42

A $C = 3d$

B $C = 5d$

C $C = 6d$

D $C = 12d$

28 **Which number would be the 12th term in the sequence described by this table?**

n	1	2	3	4
$\frac{n}{3}$	$\frac{1}{3}$	$\frac{2}{3}$	1	$1\frac{1}{3}$

F 12

G 4

H $\frac{1}{12}$

J $\frac{3}{12}$

29 **Find the area of the figure.**

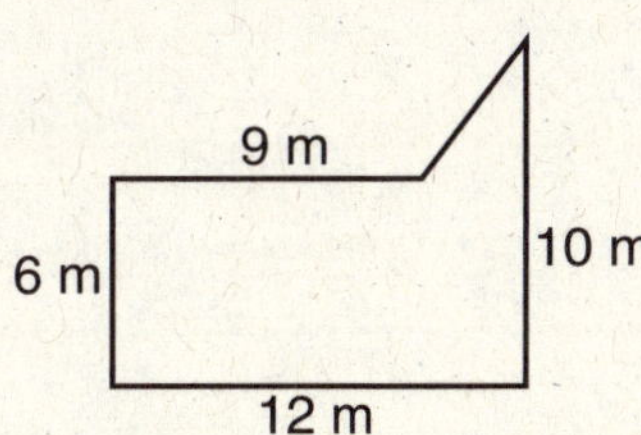

A 24 m^2

B 36 m^2

C 42 m^2

D 78 m^2

GO ON

30 Find an expression describing the rule for the sequence in the table.

Term Number (n)	1	2	3	4	5
Number in Sequence	9	10	11	12	13

F $n + 9$

G $9n$

H $8n$

J $n + 8$

31 Stan makes pins from shells and sells them for 75¢ each. How many pins would he need to sell to earn $12?

A 10 pins

B 12 pins

C 14 pins

D 16 pins

32 In a proportion, which ratio could be shown equal to $\frac{6}{7}$?

F $\frac{24}{25}$

G $\frac{18}{21}$

H $\frac{13}{14}$

J $\frac{12}{18}$

33 Jan runs at a rate of 6 miles per hour. If m = the number of miles Jan runs and h = the number of hours, find an equation to represent the number of miles she runs in h hours.

A $m = \frac{h}{6}$

B $h = 6m$

C $m = 6h$

D $h = m + 6$

34 Alex uses the formula $q = \frac{c}{4}$ to change cups (c) into quarts (q). He has 16 cups of fresh-squeezed juice. How many quarts of fresh-squeezed juice does he have?

F 4 qt

G 8 qt

H 12 qt

J 64 qt

35 Solve for x.

$-3x + 5 = -1$

A $-1\frac{1}{3}$

B -2

C 2

D -6

GO ON

Name ____________________ Class ____________ Date ____________

TerraNova Practice Test

36 **The table below represents the equation $y = -4x + 8$. Use the table to solve the related equation $0 = -4x + 8$.**

x	−2	−1	0	1	2
y	16	12	8	4	0

F $x = 0$

G $x = -2$

H $x = -8$

J $x = 2$

37 **Which shows the graph of the inequality $x \geq -7$?**

A
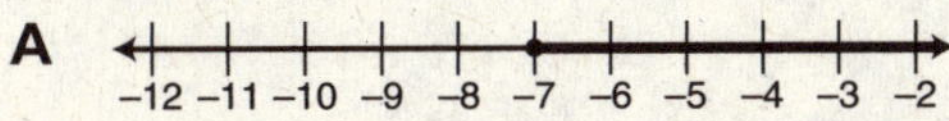

B −12 −11 −10 −9 −8 −7 −6 −5 −4 −3 −2

C −12 −11 −10 −9 −8 −7 −6 −5 −4 −3 −2

D −12 −11 −10 −9 −8 −7 −6 −5 −4 −3 −2

38 **The value of Myra's stamp collection has gone up 20% since last year. If it was worth \$450 last year, how much is it worth now?**

F \$430

G \$470

H \$540

J \$9,000

39 **Which is 4,250,000,000 written in scientific notation?**

A 0.425×10^{10}

B 4.25×10^{8}

C 4.25×10^{9}

D 425×10^{7}

40 **Find the rule for the translation of *ABCD*.**

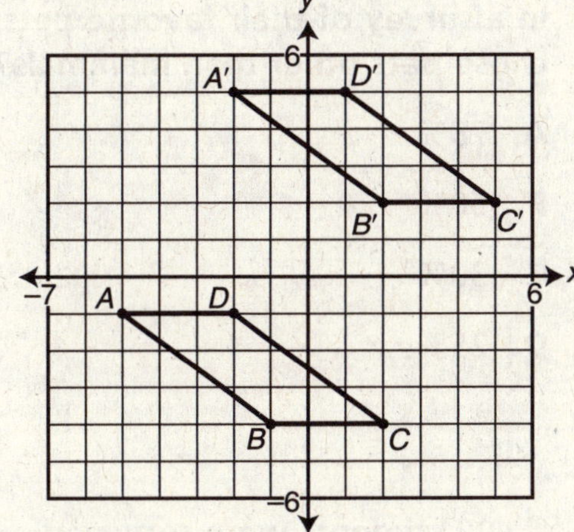

F $(x, y) \rightarrow (x + 3, y + 6)$

G $(x, y) \rightarrow (x - 3, y - 6)$

H $(x, y) \rightarrow (x + 5, y + 8)$

J $(x, y) \rightarrow (x - 5, y - 8)$

GO ON

TerraNova Practice Test

Use this graph for Items 41–43.

Fish
Birds
Other
Mammals

41 **In a survey of their favorite pets, about what percent of students chose pets other than mammals?**

A 75%

B 50%

C 30%

D 25%

42 **If 400 students were surveyed, which is the best estimate for the number choosing mammals?**

F 100

G 300

H 200

J 150

43 **About what percent of the students surveyed chose fish?**

A 90%

B 30%

C 25%

D 10%

Name ____________________ Class ____________ Date ____________

TerraNova Practice Test

44 **This stem-and-leaf diagram shows test scores for Mr. Ramirez's class. What is the class's median test score?**

Stem	Leaf
7	4 5 5 6 8
8	0 1 4 4 7
9	3 4 6

F 87

G 84

H 81

J 80

45 **The table shows the results for several rolls of two number cubes. Use the table to find the experimental probability of rolling a sum of 5.**

Rolls (Sum)	2	3	4	5	6	7	8	9	10	11	12
Frequency	1	4	5	7	10	12	6	3	5	1	2

A $\frac{1}{6}$

B $\frac{1}{8}$

C $\frac{1}{9}$

D $\frac{1}{10}$

46 **Angela spins a spinner with the numbers 1–6 on it. What is the probability that she will spin a 2 three times in a row?**

F $\frac{1}{216}$

G $\frac{1}{52}$

H $\frac{1}{36}$

J $\frac{1}{18}$

47 Which is the mean for this data set?

5, 2, 4, 40, 11, 5, 9, 6, 8

A 5.5

B 5

C 9

D 10

48 The results of a survey showed that 88% of the people would vote in favor of the town referendum to improve road conditions. Suppose 940 people vote. About how many people can you expect to vote in favor of the referendum?

F about 500

G about 827

H about 880

J about 450

49 Without looking, June picked a marble out of a bag containing 4 red, 6 blue, and 8 yellow marbles. Find the probability that the marble she picked was blue.

A $\frac{1}{6}$

B $\frac{1}{5}$

C $\frac{1}{3}$

D $\frac{1}{2}$

50 An angle measures 135°. Which of the following describes or gives the measure of a complement and a supplement of the angle?

F 45°; 45°

G no complement; 55°

H 35°; 55°

J no complement; 45°

51 $\triangle D'E'F'$ is the reflection of $\triangle DEF$ across the x-axis. Find the coordinates of the vertices of $\triangle D'E'F'$.

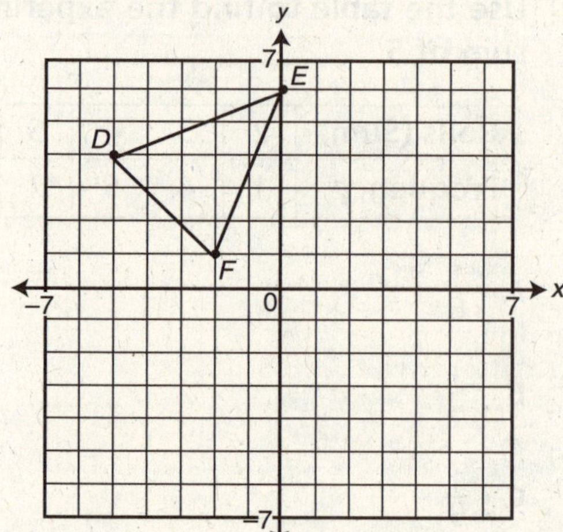

A $D'(-5, -4)$, $E'(0, -6)$ $F'(-2, -1)$

B $D'(5, -4)$, $E'(0, 6)$ $F'(2, 1)$

C $D'(5, -4)$, $E'(0, -6)$ $F'(2, -1)$

D $D'(-5, 4)$, $E'(0, 6)$ $F'(-2, 1)$

GO ON

Name ______________________ Class ______________ Date ______________

TerraNova Practice Test

52 **Which is the perimeter of the garden?**

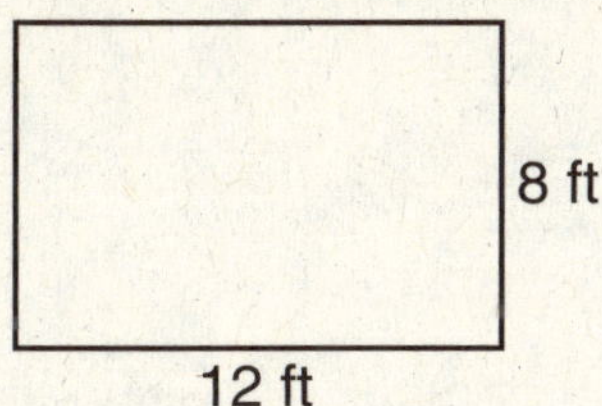

F 48 ft

G 20 ft

H 96 ft

J 40 ft

53 **Karen needs to paint the outside of the storehouse shown. She will not paint the roof. A gallon of paint covers about 400 square feet. How many gallons will she need to buy?**

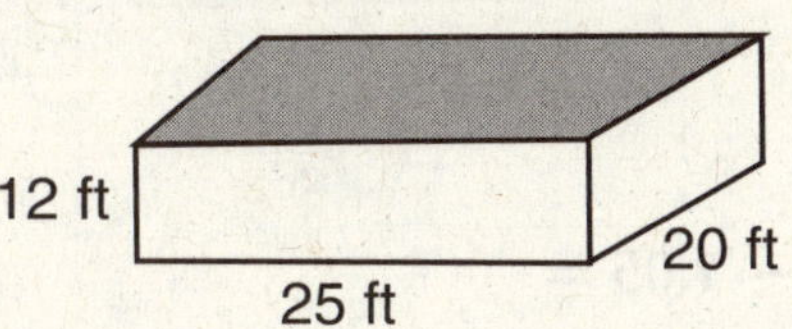

A 2 gal

B 3 gal

C 4 gal

D 5 gal

54 **Classify the triangle by its sides and by its angles.**

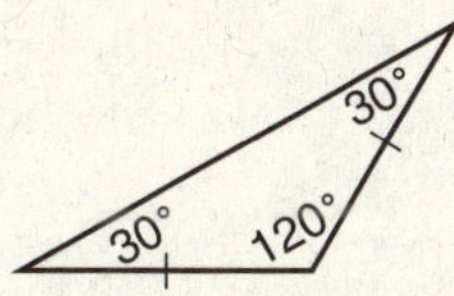

F acute scalene

G obtuse scalene

H acute isosceles

J obtuse isosceles

55 **Which of these rectangles is similar to a rectangle that measures 15 cm by 18 cm?**

A 3 cm by 6 cm

B 5 cm by 9 cm

C 10 cm by 12 cm

D 12 cm by 14 cm

56 **Use the figure to find a pair of perpendicular lines.**

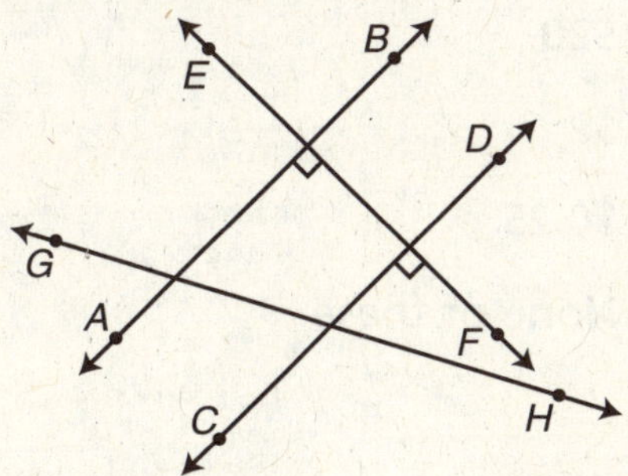

F $\overleftrightarrow{AB}$ and $\overleftrightarrow{CD}$

G $\overleftrightarrow{AB}$ and $\overleftrightarrow{GH}$

H $\overleftrightarrow{CD}$ and $\overleftrightarrow{EF}$

J $\overleftrightarrow{CD}$ and $\overleftrightarrow{GH}$

TerraNova Practice Test

Part 3

1 **38.06 + 7.3 =**

A 38.79

B 45.39

C 45.9

D 44.36

E None of these

2 **38 − (−15) =**

F 23

G 33

H 43

J 53

K None of these

3 **5% of $50 =**

A $25

B $20

C $2

D $0.25

E None of these

4 **5.6 × 0.14 =**

F 7.84

G 7.64

H 0.784

J 0.0764

K None of these

5 **65 − 20 ÷ (2 + 3) =**

A 9

B 15

C 61

D 69

E None of these

6 **6 − 1.05 =**

F 5.94

G 5.05

H 5.04

J 4.95

E None of these

GO ON

Name ______________________ Class ______________ Date ______________

TerraNova Practice Test

7 $10\frac{1}{5} - 8\frac{4}{5} =$

A $1\frac{2}{5}$

B $2\frac{3}{5}$

C $2\frac{2}{5}$

D $1\frac{3}{5}$

E None of these

8 $5\frac{3}{4} \div 1\frac{1}{3} =$

F $7\frac{2}{3}$

G $5\frac{1}{4}$

H $4\frac{5}{16}$

J $3\frac{2}{3}$

K None of these

9 $\frac{5}{21} + \frac{4}{7} =$

A $\frac{9}{28}$

B $\frac{9}{21}$

C $\frac{17}{21}$

D $\frac{6}{7}$

E None of these

10 $30 \div 0.0005 =$

F 6

G 600

H 6,000

J 60,000

K None of these

11 $\frac{21}{48} \times \frac{8}{45} =$

A $\frac{1}{10}$

B $\frac{7}{90}$

C $\frac{1}{15}$

D $\frac{7}{8}$

E None of these

12 $-50 \times 7 =$

F -35

G 300

H 350

J -350

K None of these

GO ON

13 $15 + 3(2 - 1) - 6 \div 2 =$

A 17

B 15

C 7

D 6

E None of these

14 $-56 \div (-8) =$

F −448

G 7

H −7

J 448

K None of these

15 $\frac{16 - 4}{3} \times 7 - 8 =$

A 12

B 13

C 20

D 28

E None of these

16 $26 + (-18) =$

F −44

G 8

H −8

J 44

K None of these

17 15 is 30% of what number?

A 5

B 45

C 90

D 100

E None of these

18 15% of 40 =

F $2\frac{2}{3}$

G $\frac{5}{9}$

H 6

J 60

K None of these

19 $48 - 36 \div (4 + 2) =$

A 42

B 41

C 2

D 5

E None of these

20 6 is what percent of 24?

F 20%

G 25%

H 30%

J 40%

K None of these